I am Here to Fulfill My Destiny

Boris Cho

AOS Publishing, 2025

ISBN: 978-1-998662-89-0

Cover Design: Meredith Lindsay

Visit AOS Publishing's website:
www.aospublishing.com

Dedicated to Macy Bernice Cho—

the sweetest and most beautiful daughter in all of time and space.

You will always be my princess, and I will always be your king.

Every day is a celebration of art, creativity, and connection, the very pulse that has carried me through a journey of healing, mindfulness, and gratitude. These words echo through every version of myself; past, present, and yet to be.

—Sincerely, Boris Cho

Boris Cho is a passionate writer and poet, dedicated to exploring the profound themes of love, resilience, fatherhood, values, and spirituality in his work. His collection, *I Am Here to Fulfill My Destiny — Sincerely, Boris*, is a heartfelt compilation of poetry and passages that delve into the complexities of human experience, embracing vulnerability and the quest for inner peace.

Drawing from his life experiences, Boris writes with an authenticity that resonates deeply with readers. As a devoted father, he reflects on the joys and challenges of parenting, using his role as a lens to examine growth and the transformative power of love. His words encourage readers to confront their fears, celebrate their journeys, and cultivate a sense of spirituality in their everyday lives.

Boris's poetry invites contemplation and introspection, offering insights into the human condition while fostering a sense of connection and understanding. Each piece serves as a reminder that we are all on a journey toward our destinies, and that through resilience and vulnerability, we can find the strength to navigate life's challenges. Through his work, Boris aims to inspire others to embrace their own journeys, finding solace and strength in the written word.

I Am Here To Fulfill My Destiny

For as long as I can remember, I've sought answers; about who I am, what my purpose is, and how I can contribute meaningfully to this world. Through reflection, challenges, and experiences, I've come to understand that life is not merely a series of random events, but a carefully-orchestrated journey meant to guide me toward fulfilling my highest potential. Every individual carries within them a unique blueprint, a map to their own personal destiny. This realization became a lens through which I started to see my path as more than just a pursuit of success; it was about alignment with my true self.

For much of my life, I battled with the darkness and struggles of mental health; depression and anxiety became my familiar companions. Growing up in a home that was often terrifying in its unpredictability, I felt a profound loneliness, a disconnect from the world around me. The silence between people I loved, the absence of affection, and the emotional isolation shaped my earliest experiences, making me question whether happiness was something I would ever truly know. But it is in these very struggles that I learned the most powerful lesson: it is often through the darkest moments that we uncover the greatest clarity about who we are and the journey we are destined to travel.

I've always believed that each of us has a specific design, an energetic structure that influences how we interact with the world, how we make decisions, and how we evolve. Life is not a singular straight line; it is a series of lessons designed to help us grow into the person we are meant to be. I've faced adversity: growing up as an immigrant, enduring the pain of a broken home, surviving a toxic marriage, and overcoming the challenges of losing a part of myself both physically and emotionally. These experiences weren't just obstacles; they were opportunities to refine my understanding of my own strengths and purpose.

Each challenge, each heartache, felt like a test of my endurance, of my capacity to survive. But what I now understand is that these were not punishments or mere suffering; they were part of my journey to discover the deeper truth of who I am. They pushed me to recognize my inner authority, to take ownership of my choices, and to realize that I am not at the mercy of life's chaos. I learned that to become the man, the father, the partner, the friend, and the sibling I was destined to be, I had to confront the parts of myself that were shaped by fear and loss. My past no longer defines me; it has been the fuel that drives my ambition to build a life of authenticity, compassion, and resilience.

At the heart of my journey is the notion that we are constantly co-creating our reality. The choices we make, consciously or unconsciously, align us with the greater flow of life or resist it. Every hardship I faced was a teacher, leading me back to myself, showing me that it is through self-awareness and alignment with my inner peace that I can unlock my true potential. I've learned that when I'm in tune with my personal energy, when I make decisions from a place of inner authority rather than fear or expectation, I become empowered. I've come to believe that our destinies are not about becoming someone else, but about becoming more of who we were always meant to be. I see that now in every aspect of my life: in the way I approach my career in media and advertising, in the connections I maintain with the people I love, and in the devotion I bring to fatherhood, where my daughter continually teaches me the most sacred lessons of love, patience, and resilience.

Being a single father to my beautiful and compassionate daughter has been the clearest reflection of my growth, and I've embraced my role as both a protector and a guide. She is my compass, reminding me every day of the importance of patience, to stay present, to be kind even when the world feels harsh, to love, and to see strength in vulnerability. As I show her that strength lies in kindness and resilience, I also remind myself that these qualities are essential to the person I am becoming. My journey is not just about survival anymore; it's about thriving, about becoming the best version of myself, not only for my daughter but for everyone else around me.

Every step I take toward becoming the best version of myself is rooted in the desire to set an example for her, to show her that our destinies are not set in stone but rather carved by the intention we place into the world, by the love we give and the courage we summon.

I've come to understand that the essence of life's journey is not to change who we are, but to become more of who we've always been. It's a process of uncovering, of returning

4

to that core essence, and aligning with it more fully every day. My ambition has shifted from achieving external success to internal peace, where kindness, resilience, and ambition meet to form a life that feels authentically mine.

The lessons I've gathered have taught me that I don't need to be perfect; I need to be present, in tune with my own self, and committed to living authentically. I now understand that the journey is not about external validation but about aligning with my true self, listening to the wisdom that comes from within, and living with integrity in every action, whether in my career or in the way I show up for my friends and family. Through it all, through the darkness and the light, I've found my path, my purpose.

My name is Boris Cho, and I am here to fulfill my destiny.
—Sincerely, Boris

The Act of Learning Is, In Itself, An Act Of Love; For Oneself, For Others, And For The World

While others stepped into their adult lives with degrees and institutional education, I leaned into curiosity, resourcefulness, and the need to prove that a lack of formal schooling could not define the boundaries of my potential.

My career in media and advertising became my classroom: each client challenge was a case study, each meeting an opportunity to absorb. I approached the industry like an athlete studies a playbook, mastering its nuances, anticipating its moves, and finding new ways to elevate my craft.

But learning is not just about survival; it's about flourishing. Over the years, I've come to understand that the true mastery of learning lies not in amassing information, but in knowing how to retain, apply, and integrate it meaningfully into every corner of my life.

I've learned to ask myself: What does it mean to truly *understand* something? Not just to memorize it for a fleeting purpose, but to internalize it, to let it change me? Learning, I've found, is not a single act, but a series of practices, much like meditation. It requires presence, patience, and purpose.

I have come to learn that lifelong learning starts with the right mindset. Every new skill or insight begins with belief:

belief that the effort is worthwhile, that failure is part of the process, and that growth often lies just beyond discomfort.

Early in my career, I felt the weight of imposter syndrome. Everyone around me seemed so confident, wearing their credentials like badges of honor. I had to learn that my value came not from the letters after my name, but from my ability to adapt, to grow, and to contribute in meaningful ways.

This shift in mindset became a foundation not just for professional success, but for every personal challenge I've faced since: surviving a toxic marriage, rebuilding my identity, and learning to be a father whose daughter sees strength in humility and perseverance.

There is immense power in focused attention. Learning deeply requires the discipline to focus; not just for minutes, but for sustained, meaningful stretches of time. In a world of constant distractions, this is a skill I had to cultivate. I remember times when a single pitch or client deadline demanded complete immersion. The clarity of thought that comes from deep work is incomparable; it carves pathways in the brain that shallow skimming never can.

Outside of work, I've applied this lesson to personal growth: studying Buddhism taught me the value of single-pointed attention, whether through meditation or simply listening deeply during conversations. True focus, I've realized, is an act of care, for others, and for oneself.

Through my learning journey, I have come to understand the importance of making space for repetition. One of the most practical lessons I've learned is that retention doesn't happen in one sitting. It's the repeated engagement with an idea—over days, weeks, or even years—that solidifies it in the mind. I see this now in the way I educate my daughter. We revisit lessons—not just new skills, problem solving, or reading, but values like resilience and kindness—through stories, shared experiences, and reflection.

In my professional life, this principle has shaped how I mentor colleagues. Revisiting a concept, reframing it, and finding new ways to apply it ensures that the learning sticks and evolves.

It's not enough to learn for learning's sake. Knowledge must be applied, tested, and lived. When I began studying feminism, it wasn't just to understand history or theory; it was to become a better advocate for my daughter to ensure that she grows up seeing herself as equal, capable, and deserving of every opportunity.

Similarly, my recent exploration of art therapy wasn't an academic exercise; it was a way to process my own traumas and reconnect with my curiosity and creativity after struggling through mental, physical, financial, and emotional abuse throughout a fourteen-year relationship. These applications of learning have been deeply personal, but they've also enriched how I show up for others.

Through reflection, my understanding of my past, present, and future self has deepened. Journaling, storytelling, and conversations have been my tools for reflection. After each experience, whether a professional success, a personal failure, or a moment of quiet joy, I ask: *What did I learn? How did this change me?* This habit has turned my life into a tapestry of interconnected lessons, each thread woven with intention.

This reflective practice has been particularly important in parenting. When my daughter and I discuss her day or share a moment together; I see how these small acts of reflection build her emotional intelligence and deepen our bond.

To be a better colleague, I've learned to listen without judgment, to ask questions that spark insight, and to challenge my own biases. To be a better father, I've embraced patience, the art of asking instead of telling, and the joy of rediscovering the world through a child's eyes. To be a better friend and partner, I've worked on vulnerability, on showing my flaws and trusting others with them.

But most importantly, learning has been about becoming a better version of myself. I've faced darkness; mental health struggles, professional setbacks, and personal losses; but each challenge has been a teacher, shaping the man I am today and encouraging me to become the man I am destined to become.

The rewards of this journey are immeasurable. Professionally, it's allowed me to grow into a leader who inspires and uplifts, and puts people first. Personally, it's given me tools to heal, to connect, and to thrive. As a father, it's shown me how to model resilience and curiosity for my daughter. And most of all, it's taught me that the act of learning is, in itself, an act of love: for oneself, for others, and for the world.

My journey is far from over. Whether it's delving deeper into Buddhism, expanding and honoring my commitment to feminism, honing my skills in storytelling, or simply sitting with my daughter to explore her latest curiosity, I know that each step forward brings me closer to the life I aspire to live: one of meaning, connection, and endless growth.

—Sincerely, Boris

The Act Of Self-Partnership And
Being Safe Within Myself

I used to think that love was an external pursuit, something to chase, capture, and contain; always outside of myself, dependent on the actions, approval, and love of another. In the wreckage of a toxic, fourteen-year relationship that drained me emotionally, mentally, and financially, I lived in a distorted version of attachment. I clung tightly to the belief that my worth was measured by someone else's satisfaction. Her accusations of my failures as a husband, father, and friend became the loudest voice in my head. I lost myself in her disdain, convinced I was unlovable, inadequate, perpetually unworthy. And when the weight of that truth finally broke me, I learned to retreat into silence, into avoidance: a habit born from survival. I gave less and less of myself, believing that distance would protect me. All it did was build walls so high that even I couldn't see over them.

Years later, as I sat in the uncomfortable stillness of my own solitude, I came to realize what was missing wasn't someone else; it was me. We often think attachment is about how we love others, but it's first and foremost about how we attach to ourselves. Understanding this, really internalizing it, felt like a quiet revolution. A painful but profound unraveling.

Attachment patterns—avoidant, anxious, disorganized, secure—aren't just clinical terms. They're survival maps we draw in childhood, based on the love (or lack thereof) we received. I grew up in a home where affection was absent, where fear dictated connection, where mistakes were met with punishment rather than understanding. I learned to adapt to that reality. To be perfect. To shrink myself. And later, I carried those patterns into a marriage where love was conditional, transactional. I over-gave, I overthought, I over-apologized. My anxious attachment begged for reassurance that never came, while avoidant habits numbed the pain of never feeling seen or ever being loved.

The thing about attachment that I have come to recently learn is that it doesn't just heal through others. It heals *through you.* Secure attachment begins with a radical commitment to yourself; to meet your needs, honor your boundaries, and learn the art of self-soothing. For the first time, I had to ask: *What does it mean to be securely attached to myself?* I wasn't sure. But I knew I could no longer outsource my emotional safety to another person. No relationship could fix the fractures I hadn't tended to in myself.

This is where the philosophy of self-attachment comes in. It's a quiet kind of love, built not on grand gestures but on daily, intentional acts of self-trust. I learned to recognize the voices of my past, the ones that said I was not enough, and gently separate myself from them. It wasn't easy. I had spent decades believing I was the problem. Rebuilding required learning to speak to myself with the same tenderness I would offer my daughter.

12

Self-attachment asks you to become your own safe harbor. When my anxious patterns pulled me toward over-explaining or pleasing others at my own expense, I learned to pause, to check in. *What am I feeling? What do I need?* That simple question became revolutionary. I had spent so much of my life disconnected from my needs that the act of recognizing them felt like meeting myself for the first time.

When my avoidant side pushed me to shut down, to retreat into isolation, I resisted the old urge to numb and distract. I showed up. I sat with the discomfort of vulnerability, of loneliness, of sadness; and I didn't run. Self-soothing became a recent practice: I learned to ground myself, to hold space for my emotions without judgment or escape. It felt foreign at first. Awkward. But the more I did it, the more secure I became in my own presence.

The beauty of secure attachment is that it doesn't require perfection. It's not about never feeling anxious or avoidant again. It's about noticing when those patterns show up, understanding where they came from, and lovingly guiding yourself back to center. It's about building a life where your worth isn't conditional, where you don't have to chase love or hide from it. You simply *are.* And in that wholeness, you are enough.

Being self-partnered isn't loneliness. It's liberation. It's learning to love yourself with the patience you were never given. It's giving yourself the safety that was denied to you. For me, that meant reimagining relationships; not as sources of validation or escape, but as spaces where I could show up as my full, secure self. That didn't mean rejecting love; on the contrary, it meant preparing to love and be loved deeply, without the desperation of needing someone else to "complete" me.

I've come to understand that secure attachment isn't a destination; it's a practice. It's a daily commitment to yourself; to hold your hand through the messy, imperfect moments and whisper: *You're safe. I've got you.* And when you learn to be that for yourself, everything else changes. You stop settling for less. You stop chasing people who can't meet you where you are. You begin to choose connection over control, boundaries over burnout, self-compassion over self-sacrifice.

If I could speak to the man I was all those years ago, the one who believed his worth was tied to his ability to endure, I would tell him this: You don't have to be the hero of someone else's chaos. You are not unlovable because you were unloved. Healing begins with you. You are your own home.

And now, in this quiet space of my life—self-partnered, rebuilding, healing—I know what it means to feel secure. It isn't a guarantee that life will be easy or love will be perfect. But it is profound knowing that, no matter what happens, I am enough. I am whole. I am safe within myself.

For the first time, I am free.
—Sincerely, Boris

What Stoicism Taught Me

For much of my life, I carried the weight of a past I could not change. I grew up in a home filled with fear and uncertainty, where affection was scarce and mistakes seemed unforgivable. Later, I endured fourteen years in a toxic marriage, losing myself in a storm of manipulation and emotional pain. When it finally ended, I was left to rebuild not only my sense of self, but also a safe and loving environment for my daughter. I have faced grief, anxiety, and depression, all of which grew louder in the silence of those dark chapters. And yet, through these trials; and the near-death reckoning of brain aneurysms; I have come to understand that peace cannot be found in the shifting winds of circumstance, but only in the stillness of the soul.

Stoicism taught me that much. It is a philosophy rooted not in lofty ideals but in the gritty reality of life's hardships. The Stoics remind us that suffering is inevitable, but how we respond to it is entirely within our control. This idea was a revelation for me. I realized that while I could not change the abuses of my childhood or the betrayals of my marriage, I could choose to release their grip on me. They were events; just facts, as the Stoics might say. What gave them power over me was my interpretation of them, my attachment to what I thought they meant about my worth.

The practice of *amor fati,* or loving one's fate, became my most recent anchor. It is not about resignation, but rather acceptance. When I think of my divorce, I no longer see it as fourteen wasted years but as the path that led me to the father I am today. My daughter, who teaches me resilience and compassion daily, exists because of that imperfect union. My aneurysms, terrifying as they were, stripped life to its barest essentials. They forced me to confront my mortality and to cherish the simple, fleeting joys; my daughter's laughter, the warmth of a friend's embrace, the courage to begin again.

Another cornerstone of Stoicism is the concept of the dichotomy of control: the discipline to focus on what is within my power and to release what is not. This was a hard lesson, especially in co-parenting after the divorce. I cannot control how others behave or what they think of me, but I can control how I show up; for my daughter, for myself. I can choose patience over anger, understanding over resentment. Each choice, no matter how small, builds the foundation of inner peace.

I've also come to embrace the idea of *memento mori,* to remember that we all must die. It is not morbid; it is clarifying. When I reflect on the aneurysms, I see them as reminders that time is finite, that every moment matters. Instead of fearing death, I use it as a guide to live with intention. It's why I invest in meaningful conversations with my daughter, savor the quiet pride of a job well done, and let go of bitterness that no longer serves me.

Stoicism doesn't promise happiness in the conventional sense. It doesn't shield us from pain, loss, or disappointment. What it does is offer a framework; a way to navigate life's chaos with grace and integrity. For me, it has been a map back to myself. It has taught me that I am not defined by my past, my fears, or even my failures. I am defined by how I choose to meet them. And in that choice lies freedom.

—Sincerely, Boris

Change Begins With Love And Ends In Freedom

In my journey as a father, I have come to appreciate the profound interplay between masculinity and feminism, two forces often misunderstood as opposing but which, in truth, are deeply intertwined. Raising my spirited nine-year-old daughter has made this understanding both urgent and intimate. I see the questions in her bright eyes, her quiet determination to navigate a world that does not always favor her, and I feel the weight of my role in shaping a future where she can thrive; unapologetic, unburdened, and unbound by the limits of societal expectations.

Feminism, I've realized, is not a challenge to masculinity but rather its complement, offering a lens through which our shared humanity becomes clearer. To embrace it is to deepen our collective understanding, to confront privilege without shame, and to extend empathy as a bridge between differences. As I teach my daughter about respect and equality, I encourage her to see the world not only through her own eyes but also through the eyes of others, understanding both the struggles women face and the unspoken pressures placed upon men. This dual awareness fosters a balance where all genders can flourish.

The extraordinary women in my life have been my greatest teachers in understanding how I can show up and be a supportive ally: Mentors who guided me with wisdom, a sister whose resilience inspires me, colleagues who challenged and elevated me, and friends whose strength and grace embody the courage it takes to reshape the world. They have shown me that liberation is not merely an abstract ideal but a lived practice; a daily act of courage, care, and connection that transforms everyone it touches.

Their stories, and my daughter's unfolding one, have taught me that equity requires more than admiration or education. It demands action. I must unlearn the biases I inherited, redefine love as a force for transformation, and actively contribute to dismantling the interconnected systems of oppression that stifle our potential. True liberation cannot exclude anyone; it must honor every voice, embrace every struggle, and envision a world where my daughter's humanity—and that of all women—is celebrated rather than questioned.

To create this world, I am redefining traditional gender roles within my home, encouraging my daughter to explore her passions free from the weight of convention. I aim to nurture her belief that she can forge any path, regardless of whether it aligns with societal norms. This empowerment is essential not only to her independence and resilience but also to her capacity to challenge stereotypes and advocate for herself and others.

As I reflect on these lessons, I see that this journey is not mine alone. It is a collective effort; a tapestry woven from love, strength, and shared purpose. Looking into my daughter's eyes, I am reminded that the work begins with us, with the choices we make daily to foster understanding, support, and empowerment. Change begins with love and ends in freedom.

Equity is not just an aspiration but a necessity, a vision of a world where every individual is valued for who they are, where collaboration replaces competition, and where justice is not an ideal but a reality. By embracing this philosophy, I hope to nurture a future leader who will navigate life with wisdom, empathy, and strength, carrying forward the torch of transformation that will illuminate the path for generations to come.

—Sincerely, Boris

My Commitment To Feminism (and My Daughter)

Believing in equality for women is not simply an intellectual positioning I take; it is a moral obligation. Women deserve the same political, social, and economic rights as men, not as an act of charity, but as a reflection of their inherent humanity. This is not about diminishing men to raise women, but about correcting an imbalance that has gone unquestioned for far too long.

As a man, I ask myself: How can I actively contribute to the ongoing struggle for women's rights, not as an outsider, but as a true ally?

First, I must educate myself. The history of women's fight for equality is long, complex, and ongoing. It is my responsibility to understand that history, as well as the issues women face today. This knowledge is not passive; it informs how I interact with the world and shapes the actions I take.

Second, I must listen. Truly listen. Not with the intent to respond, but with the intent to understand. The experiences of women in my life—my colleagues, friends, family, and especially my daughter—are the foundation of my learning. Through their stories, I gain insight into the barriers they face, and through their struggles, I find where my voice and actions can be of value.

Third, I must not be a bystander. Whether it's in a workplace, a public setting, or even within my own community, I have a responsibility to stand up against violence or discrimination when it occurs. Silence perpetuates injustice. I cannot remain indifferent to the suffering of others, especially when my inaction would contribute to it.

Lastly, I must challenge the systems and mindsets around me, particularly among fellow men. I have a unique opportunity to engage in conversations that might feel uncomfortable but are necessary. When I speak against sexist attitudes, I'm not just correcting the behavior of others; I'm reinforcing a new standard for how we treat each other as human beings. It's a small but significant way of reshaping the world for my daughter and for the women who will come after her.

This is more than a call to action. It is a promise, a commitment I make to myself; to continuously grow, to question my own biases, to become the kind of man who contributes to a more just and equal world.

And it is a promise to my daughter that I will strive to be an example of the respect, understanding, and compassion that all women deserve. In doing so, I hope to leave her a world better than the one I inherited, a world where her worth will never be in question.

—Sincerely, Boris

For Her, I Am Whole, And In Her, I Am Healed

There are parts within me that have been shaped by early pain and fear; a life spent on guard, vigilant against the consequences of any misstep. I learned to divide myself, to hide certain parts, for safety's sake, leaving fragments of myself that grew accustomed to survival, even as I yearned for connection. But in time, I have come to understand that this fractured past within me holds potential for healing, for growth, and, perhaps most importantly, for a new way of being.

These inner divisions—the parts of myself that I once rejected, feared, or simply didn't understand—are not obstacles to overcome but parts of me that require compassion and understanding. They formed in a space of need, a response to an environment that offered little safety. Each part—the cautious one, the silent one, the fierce protector—emerged in response to that fearful environment. Rather than erasing them, I now see the importance of recognizing and holding space for these parts, welcoming them as survivors who kept me whole when wholeness felt impossible. Recognizing them as such has shifted my inner perspective; I now see them not as burdens but as bearers of survival, protectors who were once essential and who still seek my recognition and care.

In parenting my daughter, I see these fragmented parts come to life in unexpected ways. The father I have become is one forged in the fires of my own longing to be held, understood, and valued. Every hug, every kind word, every act of support I offer her is an affirmation of the love I once sought. In her presence, I am able to rewrite the script of my own life, to give what was missing, and in doing so, heal some of the wounds that linger within. Through her, I am learning that these parts of myself do not need to be banished; they need to be invited in, to be heard, and to be allowed to rest.

There is a quiet transformation that happens when I approach these parts of myself not with disdain or shame, but with gentle curiosity. I am learning to sit with the parts of me that flinch or recoil, to hear their voices without judgment. In doing so, I become whole, not by silencing these voices but by honoring their role in my journey. This process—an intimate and, at times, unsettling path—reveals that healing is less about "fixing" oneself than it is about integration, about making room for all that I am, even the painful pieces that I once tried so hard to forget.

In becoming a father who breaks the cycles of silence and abandonment, I find myself embracing a deeper, more profound truth: That each of these parts has a place, and each is worthy of love. I am piecing myself together in a way I wish had been modeled for me as a child, building within me the compassion I once desperately needed and am now able to extend outward. My daughter, in her innocence and wisdom, is both my greatest joy and my mirror; she shows me the parts of myself that still need my love. And in loving her, I am, at last, learning to love all of me.

—

Born into darkness,
I learned to be small,
to tiptoe through childhood,
make myself quiet, unseen.

Now I carry the scars—
not as burden but as strength,
fuel for a steady, unbreaking love,
a light my daughter will never fear.

I break the silence through resilience,
rewrite the script with gentle hands.
What I was denied,
She will know as her birthright.

For her, I am whole,
and in her, I am healed.

—Sincerely, Boris

A Father's Journey In Buddhism

Once, there was a man who felt lost in the midst of his life's responsibilities and uncertainties. He had spent years chasing success, relationships, and fleeting moments of happiness, but something was always missing. Deep down, he longed for answers, for a way to navigate life with more clarity and peace. At the center of his world was his nine-year-old daughter, a bright and curious soul who brought light to his life. She was his greatest joy and his greatest motivation to find answers; to become a man who could guide her through the challenges that lay ahead.

He began his search by turning inward, realizing that he had never truly been present in his own life. He had always been running toward the next goal or worrying about the past. It was mindfulness that first opened his eyes; he learned to sit quietly and observe his thoughts, letting them pass without judgment. By practicing awareness, he began to truly see the world around him, moment by moment, for the first time. He felt the ground beneath his feet and heard the sound of his breath, and with each passing day, his mind became less scattered, more centered.

It was through mindfulness that he truly learned to savour his time with his daughter. Whether it was sharing stories before bed or listening to her laughter as she played, he practiced being there, fully engaged, letting the weight of the world fade into the background.

As his awareness grew, he started to grasp the idea of impermanence. Everything in life, he saw, was constantly changing. His emotions, his relationships, his experiences, his daughter; all of them came and went like passing cars on a busy highway. Where once he felt frustrated by loss and change, he now began to accept them as natural. This realization allowed him to let go of his attachments to things, people, and outcomes. He no longer needed everything to go his way in order to feel at peace.

He came to understand and realize that his daughter would not stay young forever; her childhood was passing by, moment by moment. Instead of fearing this truth, he embraced it, knowing that every phase of her life was precious. He wanted to show her that change was not something to be feared, but to be accepted with grace—a natural part of growing up. It was through this acceptance that he began to let go of his need to control, finding peace in the flow of life.

This led him to the concept of non-attachment. He understood now that much of his suffering came from holding onto things that were never meant to last. By loosening his grip, he felt a new sense of freedom. He could still love, still care deeply, but without the need to control or possess. In releasing his attachments, he found that he suffered less, and joy could flow more freely into his life.

Learning the lesson of non-attachment, he understood that his role as her father was to guide his daughter, not to cling to her. One day she would grow, spread her wings, and explore the world on her own. Rather than holding on tightly, he wanted to love her fully while giving her the space to become whoever she was meant to be. This shift brought him peace, knowing that love didn't mean possession; it meant support and freedom.

Along the way, he discovered the power of compassion. He realized that he had been harsh with himself for years, setting impossible standards and punishing himself when he fell short. But as he was kinder toward himself, he found it easier to extend kindness to others. The more compassionate he became, the more connected he felt to the world around him, especially to his daughter. He began to see the pain in others' lives, recognizing that everyone was struggling in their own way, and his heart opened. Compassion became a guiding principle in how he parented. When his daughter struggled or made mistakes, he responded with kindness and understanding, knowing that these were part of her growth.

But the most profound shift came when he began to question the very nature of the self. He had spent his life building an identity; his career, his achievements, the image he projected to the world. Yet through his journey, he realized that this self he had constructed was fluid, ever-changing. His ego was not a fixed thing, but rather a collection of thoughts, experiences, and beliefs that shifted over time. By letting go of the rigid idea of who he thought he was, he opened himself to growth and transformation. Through this transformation, he wanted to teach his daughter that she wasn't confined to the labels society might place on her. Like him, she was also fluid, always growing and changing. By understanding this, his daughter could remain open to new possibilities and not be burdened by the expectations of others.

The man also realized that suffering was an inevitable part of life, for both him and his daughter. It was not something to be avoided or denied, but rather something to be understood. Suffering was a part of the human experience, but by confronting its causes—desire, attachment, and ignorance—he could learn to live with greater peace.

This understanding didn't mean his life would be without pain, but it gave him tools to face suffering with grace and resilience. He hoped to show his daughter that suffering was not something to avoid, but something to confront with courage, knowing that it, too, could lead to growth.

Through meditation, the man found a daily practice that grounded him. His daily practice of meditation became a cornerstone of his journey. Each morning, before his daughter woke up, he would sit in stillness, finding peace in the quiet moments before the day began. In the stillness, he learned to quiet the noise of the world and listen to the deeper truths within himself. Meditation became his refuge, a place where he could reconnect with his breath, his mind, and his heart. It was here, in this quiet practice, that the answers he sought began to emerge; not from outside of him, but from within, and it was a gift he hoped to pass down to his daughter one day. He imagined sitting beside her as she learned to steady her mind and connect with her inner self, teaching her how to find calm in the midst of life's uncertainties.

His journey was not about reaching some distant enlightenment, but rather learning to walk through life with more clarity, compassion, and presence. His journey was also about becoming a better father. He didn't seek enlightenment for himself alone; he wanted to live in a way that would inspire his daughter. He learned that the answers he found were not just for him, but for her as well, so that one day she, too, could walk a path of mindfulness, compassion, and inner peace. His greatest hope was that, when the time came, he could pass down the wisdom he had gained, showing her that the key to happiness was not in the things they accumulated, but in how they learned to live, love, and let go.

The man's path through Buddhism showed him that the answers he sought were not in achieving or accumulating, but in letting go, in being present, and in cultivating peace within himself. And so, with each day, he continued on this path; not toward a destination, but into a deeper understanding of life as it unfolded around him and his daughter. He had found his answers, not in what he gained, but in how he continues to learn to be.

Amituofo.

–

Today, I release what no longer holds me;
I release those who have drifted away,
and those who stir doubts in my heart.

Today, I choose happiness. I step away from the shadows of toxicity, freeing myself from the burdens I've carried for far too long. I offer myself the love I so easily give to others, and in that love, I stop the quiet hurt within.

I follow the path of positivity, no longer sinking in the well of my own sorrow. I open my heart wide, letting down the walls I've built to protect what's inside. I accept my flaws and let them shape my growth.

Today, I choose healing. I forgive myself for the times I stumbled.
Today, I step forward with courage.
Today, I walk away from places I have outgrown.
Today, I cherish the gift of my own time.
Today, I choose love for myself.

—Sincerely, Boris

Cultivating Peace

I've come to realize that the mind holds immense potential for healing, far more than we often acknowledge. Instead of searching for relief solely in external solutions, I've learned to turn inward, recognizing that the tools for managing pain, stress, and anxiety already exist within me. By consciously working with the mind and body, we can shift our experience of suffering and cultivate peace.

The breath is one of the most effective means of cultivating peace. It serves as a direct link to the present, anchoring my awareness in the here and now. Through simple, controlled breathing, I can calm my nervous system and influence my subconscious mind. This process is not only about relaxation; it's about retraining the mind to respond differently to stress and discomfort. With every mindful breath, I've gained a greater sense of control over my emotional and physical states.

Mindfulness is another critical practice. By observing my thoughts and emotions without immediately reacting to them, I've developed a new perspective on pain and stress. Rather than seeing these as threats to be resisted, I now view them as signals, indicators that something in me needs attention. Mindfulness allows me to approach these signals with curiosity and compassion, which can reduce their intensity and help me respond more thoughtfully.

In this process, meditation plays a key role. It gives me access to the deeper parts of my subconscious, where my past experiences and emotional patterns are stored. Through regular meditation, I've been able to reshape my responses to stress and pain, moving away from automatic reactions that increase suffering. Meditation has taught me that healing is a process of aligning the mind and body toward peace, not by force but through consistent, patient practice.

I no longer feel powerless in the face of external stressors. By focusing on my inner world—my thoughts, my breath, and my awareness—I've developed a sense of resilience that isn't easily shaken by outside circumstances. Healing, I've learned, is an ongoing journey. Each day offers a new opportunity to practice these skills, to remind myself that while pain or anxiety may arise, I have the ability to transform how I experience them.

—

Each morning, I rise to greet the day,
Read words of wisdom to light my way.
With visions clear and actions aligned,
I center my soul, in peace I find.

Meditation whispers, "Be still, be strong,"
And in the silence, I belong.
Writing my truths, I set them free;
A life of growth that belongs to me.

Afternoons slow, with a gentle breeze—
Books and thoughts, no need to please.
Turning off screens, I reclaim the hour.
In quiet moments, I find my power.

A podcast hums, a guiding sound,
New ideas grow, deep and profound.
As evening falls, I move and I breathe,
Walking the path where my heart is pleased.

With words once more, I let them flow,
A reflection of where I long to go.
In the stillness, I find my light,
And greet the peace that comes each night.

I promise to hold my routine with care,
To nourish my body, to breathe fresh air.
Move every day, let my muscles sing,
Phone set aside, to let nature ring.

Carry my camera, to capture the skies,
Saving each dollar, with mindful eyes.
Sober, present, embracing the new,
Writing forever, my heart's truth in view.

In this journey, I grow and unfold,
A story of strength, resilience and bold.

—Sincerely, Boris

The Ability to Rise:
I Am More Than My Circumstances

Life has never been a gentle teacher to me. It has tested the boundaries of my spirit with relentless precision, introducing me to fear, doubt, and despair at an age when innocence should have prevailed. I grew up in a house where love was a foreign language, its silence broken only by the sharpness of anger or indifference. As the years unfolded, I found myself trapped in a marriage devoid of tenderness, a slow erosion of self over fourteen long years. I emerged from it scarred but resolute, carrying the weight of a broken heart and the joy of fatherhood in equal measure. My daughter became my guiding star, a reminder that healing is both a necessity and a duty.

Yet healing is neither linear nor kind. It demands resilience, a mental toughness that does not deny pain but rather transforms it. This resilience begins, I've learned, by mastering one's thoughts. In the face of adversity, the mind often conspires against us, magnifying fears, feeding anxieties, and breeding self-doubt. But just as the body can be trained to endure, so too can the mind be fortified. I have discovered that this is not an act of suppression but of discipline—a quiet insistence on reframing challenges as opportunities and setbacks as lessons.

Emotions, particularly the darker ones, are persistent companions. Depression and anxiety often cloud my path, whispering that I am not enough, that I will falter. But I have learned to face these voices with clarity and grace. Negative emotions, I've come to understand, are not enemies to be vanquished but signals to be interpreted. Acknowledging their presence without succumbing to their grip has been liberating, an act of courage that requires daily practice.

Equally, I have learned the importance of self-awareness, of pausing amidst chaos to ask: What am I truly feeling? What do I truly need? These questions have helped me navigate the complexities of single fatherhood, where the demands of nurturing another life often leave little room for my own. Yet, in showing up for my daughter, I have found strength in consistency and clarity in purpose.

Adversity, I now realize, is not life's punishment but its crucible. It forges character, sharpens resolve, and reveals the depths of our courage. There is no shame in struggle; it is the soil from which resilience grows. This journey has taught me that vulnerability is not a weakness but a profound strength; a doorway to authenticity and connection.

Healing, I know now, is a practice, not a destination. It is in the small rituals of care: The decision to show up for myself, the grace to forgive my past, and the resolve to keep moving forward, no matter how slowly. Each step is a quiet rebellion against despair, a declaration that I am more than my circumstances.

Through this lens, I no longer see my trials as tragedies but as gifts wrapped in difficult lessons. The journey has not been easy, but it has been worth it. For in the end, the resilience I have cultivated is not just for me; it is for my daughter, who watches me navigate this life with courage and poise. I hope she learns, as I have, that strength is not the absence of struggle, but the ability to rise despite it.

—Sincerely, Boris

My Friend, The Healer

We grew up in the same small town,
summers brushing by like strangers.
One day you came by during band practice
and wrote down the titles of my CD collection,
and I smiled.

Years later, we crossed paths in Toronto;
you, studying to heal others,
We never named what we were.
Sleepovers, meals shared,
your love for my cat, our weekends together.

I think of you sometimes,
your voice from Europe, the music in bed,
your quirky and dorky self, so unguarded.
And though we've drifted,

I know you're well;
still carrying that quiet grace,
living the life you deserve.

—Sincerely, Boris

A Haiku: For Kitty Boy

You were a handsome
orange and white tabby cat
majestic and loved.

—Sincerely, Boris

Streetcars

The streetcars come and go,
Unbound by time,
Rolling with a will of their own,
Arriving only when they please.

The conductor is merely a piece of the machine;
Like the tracks, the brakes, the doors,
An anonymous pulse in the city's flow.
Doors hiss open, bodies spill out,

Others flood in, filling the narrow aisle.
Some lucky, seated;
The rest, swaying, clinging to metal poles,
Suspended between stops.

Each rider locked in their own world,
Eyes averted, hands clutching bags or phones,
Ears drowned in playlists of morning commutes.
We are, for now, silent travelers,
Bound together by a single, fleeting purpose:
Destination.

—Sincerely Boris

A Haiku: Fortune Cookie

Wisdom lurks inside,
A fortune-telling cookie,
Cracked, crumbled, untold.

—Sincerely, Boris

The Fragility Of Trust And The Echo of Dishonesty

Trust begins within. It is an intimate act of self-awareness, a journey of learning to listen to the voice inside, of refining intuition until it feels like an unshakable compass. To trust others, we must first cultivate trust in ourselves—a quiet confidence that our choices, no matter how uncertain, are guided by something deeper, something true. This self-trust is the foundation upon which all other connections rest.

But trust with others is more delicate. It is earned slowly, built through small acts of consistency, vulnerability, and presence. It is fragile, a currency of the heart that requires both patience and persistence. Yet, in the blink of an eye, it can vanish. A single lie, a fleeting betrayal, or even the weight of silence can shatter what took years to nurture. Like glass, once broken, trust rarely returns to its original form. Even in the painstaking process of rebuilding, the cracks remain visible, forever altering its shape.

There is another way trust fades: the slow erosion caused by distance. In time, even without betrayal, trust can slip through our fingers, lost in the space between absence and silence. The image of the person we once trusted morphs, shifts, and no longer resembles the one we held close. Distance, both emotional and physical, can sever the bond, leaving us questioning the very foundation of what was once certain.

Trust, then, is more than a feeling; it is a sacred state of mind. It is a neural symphony, signaling when to lean in and when to step back, when to open our hearts and when to protect them. It shapes our behavior, guiding our actions like an invisible hand.

Cherish the trust you place in others as if it were a tender flame, vulnerable to even the softest breeze. Protect it, nurture it, and do not fear letting go when it no longer feels safe. Your trust is precious, a reflection of how you wish to be held in this world. Trust your instincts; they are the guardians of your soul's deepest desires.

—

Your words once bloomed in light, sincere,
A stream of truth we both could hear.
Now they shout of whispering cries,
Drenched in dishonesty, not afraid to lie.

You spoke with heart, each word I've longed,
Honesty, bold, unbroken, and strong.
But when did deceit begin to rise?
When did truth crumble beneath the lies?

The lies wear honesty's disguise,
Sweet poison hidden in your eyes.
And with each word, you drift away;
A stranger now, who once vowed to stay.

Trust is a fragile thing to break,
A bitter pill I've learned to take.
Now silence lingers in its wake,
For all that's left feels cold and fake.

What's left to say when the truth is gone?
The dialogue between us now feels wrong.
So here I stand, beneath your lies,
Watching trust fading, as it dies.

—Sincerely, Boris

Liberation From Destructive Patterns

I have learned that much of the pain in our world stems from a system that teaches men to disconnect from their emotions. I am beginning to understand that this conditioning, rooted in patriarchy, compels men to equate strength with emotional suppression and dominance, while vulnerability is seen as weakness. As I reflect on these destructive patterns, I see how it harms not just men, but everyone around them, distorting relationships and stifling love.

I am realizing that true liberation, for both men and women, requires breaking free from these destructive patterns. It is not enough to simply reject patriarchy on an intellectual level; I must also recognize the emotional toll it takes on men, who are conditioned to shut down their feelings and distance themselves from empathy. I have come to see that, without emotional openness, without the freedom to feel and express tenderness, men remain trapped, unable to experience love in its fullness.

I have learned that healing requires more than dismantling external structures; it calls for a radical rethinking of masculinity. I am now convinced that men must be encouraged to embrace emotional vulnerability, to reconnect with their capacity for love and empathy. I understand that love, in its most profound sense, is transformative, and that it thrives when we allow ourselves to be open, honest, and unafraid of intimacy.

In this process of unlearning, I am reminded that the path to healing is not solitary. I have realized the importance of creating spaces where men can safely explore their emotions, where they can reconnect with the parts of themselves they have been taught to hide. I am committed to fostering communities that prioritize emotional growth and reject the outdated notions of control and dominance that have long defined masculinity.

I have come to believe that change is not only possible but necessary. It requires me, and all of us, to embrace new ways of being that honor emotional expression and nurture the kind of love that allows us to grow. I am committed to this journey, knowing that it holds the potential to reshape our world into one where love, justice, and connection can flourish.

—

In a world where men must not reveal
the wounds that fester deep inside,
I see now, to heal, we must unseal
the softness that we've been denied.

The path is not for men to dominate,
but to embrace what makes us whole;
to find the grace in open hands
and free us from our guarded souls.

In this, I trust, there is a way
where justice, love, and truth align.
Through courage, we can clear the way
and let our hearts entwine.

—Sincerely, Boris

A Perfect Harmony

Her intellect, an endless well of curiosity, unfolds in layers; always surprising, ever-wise. She carries a calm like the wind, her words a soothing balm to every encounter. Her presence sends ripples through my mind, lingering in the frequencies of my thoughts long after we part.

In her eyes, I see myself most clearly, my reflection brighter the nearer we stand. Those glass-like eyes, piercing and full of depth, bring me clarity with every inch we close.

Her touch, a quiet force, is healing as it moves through me. It is soft and intentional, pulling me deeper into her embrace, where I never want to leave.

Her lips glisten like a secret waiting to be shared, and I'm drawn to them, wanting nothing more than to taste the moment between us.

Her voice, recognizable even from across the room, is a melody that lingers. She is a perfect harmony, a song etched into the fabric of my being, whispering of times when life was clear, pure, and full of promise.

She wears sweaters and glasses, her hair often tied in a bun. Her smile carries echoes of a younger time, an innocence and depth intertwined. Yet every day, her beauty surpasses; not because of how she looks, but because of how effortlessly she inhabits herself, as if her presence is a kind of art no one else could recreate.

She is sharp, radiant, and endlessly fun. Her life, her own masterpiece in progress, is the most beautiful work of art I've ever known. A proud and fearless bisexual woman, she moves through the world with unapologetic authenticity, her values etched deeply into every choice she makes. Her open heart, unwavering integrity, and belief in living life as her truest self has inspired me to embrace the same.

She loves with a patient passion, a devotion that history could take notes on. To know her is to want to know her endlessly; her beauty inside and out, a universe I could explore forever.

She is everything beauty aspires to be; her courage, her values, and her love, all a beacon of light.

She is the most beautiful woman in existence, radiant in mind, body, and soul.

—

She sees the world through a prism of light;
Her vision is vast, her heart and mind open wide.
Bisexual and bold, she stands in her truth,
Generous, thoughtful, with kindness inside.

She embraces each soul for who they are,
Honoring difference, sexuality, and being proud.
For what truly matters is love's quiet truth;
Not the bodies we cherish, but hearts allowed.

Her sexuality is not her whole name,
It's how she welcomes, accepts, and defends,
Finding beauty in every path crossed,
Shielding those who need her gentle hands.

The world needs more of her radiant grace,
For we would be better with hearts like hers in place.

—Sincerely, Boris

La Belle Province

We had known each other for just ten days
When I booked our flights to Montreal.
Four nights passed in a dream,
And by the end, love quietly found us.

Six months together felt like a lifetime,
Until I let it slip from my grasp.
Two months without you stretched on,
And I unraveled for countless more.

A year has now passed since we first met,
Yet every moment is filled with your absence.
A year since I last held love in my hands;
And I would wait a lifetime to hold it again.

—Sincerely, Boris

Freckles

I used to connect each freckle with kisses,
Creating a new piece of art across your body;
Mapping out a different route each time
to get slowly closer to your destination.

—Sincerely, Boris

Aneurysms: On Borrowed Time

I am fortunate to have been given a second chance at life. After experiencing the same persistent headache every night for five consecutive days, I recognized that something was not right. Upon arriving at the hospital, the staff noticed a concerning spike in my blood pressure, prompting a CT scan of my brain.

The results revealed the presence of two aneurysms, and the medical team needed to determine whether they were ruptured or hemorrhaged. After three painful attempts at a spinal tap, I insisted that the surgeon take over.

Unfortunately, the procedure confirmed my worst fears; there was blood in the cerebrospinal fluid, indicating a hemorrhage. Faced with the grim reality of being given only a one-in-three chance of survival, I was urged to contact my family. In that moment, my thoughts were consumed by my daughter, brother, and sister: My entire world.

I awoke two days post-surgery and spent the next fourteen days recovering in the hospital. This harrowing experience profoundly altered my perspective, illuminating the areas of my life that I had neglected: My mental, physical, and spiritual health. I was forced to confront a haunting possibility: A future where my daughter would grow up without me by her side. The weight of that realization was overwhelming.

I am grateful to be here today, having narrowly escaped what felt like my expiration date last April. My daughter and I cherish every moment together, and I approach life with renewed purpose. Since my recovery, I have navigated the complexities of life, experiencing love, heartbreak, and the joys of watching my daughter thrive in fourth grade. I have been rediscovering the beauty of my city and striving to prioritize my well-being through healthier choices that benefit my mind, body, and soul.

Yet I live with the awareness that I am on borrowed time; a gift not everyone receives. Each day feels like an undeserved grace, a reminder that life is fleeting and precious, and I will never take a moment for granted. This journey has pushed me to not just survive, but to thrive with intention. I am proud of the inner work I have embraced: Mindfulness, meditation, journaling, and writing poetry, each practice helping me deepen my understanding of self and guiding me toward emotional clarity. I've rekindled my love for reading, finding solace and inspiration in the written word once more. And physically, I've committed myself to healthier living, nourishing my body through balanced nutrition and daily exercise.

This dedication to my mental and physical health has been transformative. It is a testament to my resilience and to the hard-fought battles I wage daily to become the best version of myself. I am proud of the progress I have made, and I honor this borrowed time by continuing to grow, knowing that every breath, every step forward, is a victory.

—

I walk among the living, yet I feel
the dark of those who left, who lean in close,
their soft whispers like petals falling.
The day of death; today, I feel them near,
those gone and yet alive in every breath I take.
They know I stood close, brushed the calm brink,
my life offered, a fragile cord severed,
but then stitched back with thread of borrowed breath.
They gave me seconds spun from their own stillness,
a kindness of the dead to the dying.
In their silence, I hear a call to love and live,
Not with the fury of a man cheated from death,
but with the gentleness of one held tenderly
by unseen faces, those who walk the other side,
yet send their light across to warm my face.
I am a guest here, held by the mercy of the lost,
a witness who owes his heartbeat to their generosity.
For every hour given, I bow to them, thankful.
In each sunrise, I see them wink from the shadows,
their gift of borrowed time; a vow I carry forward.

—Sincerely, Boris

Aging With Grace

At forty-one, having lived through various transitions—born in São Paulo, immigrating to Canada at the age of five, growing up in an often unhappy home, enduring a long and difficult marriage that ended in divorce, and now raising my nine-year-old daughter as a single father—I've been compelled to reflect on what it means to grow older with grace. Life has already taught me the weight of loss and the fragility of existence: The loss of my left eye to glaucoma, the two brain aneurysms I survived, and the heartache that comes from broken relationships. Yet these experiences have not only scarred me; they've also shaped me.

I've come to realize that aging gracefully isn't simply about outward appearance or clinging to youth. It's a deeper reckoning with time, a quiet acceptance of the changes within and around us. As I navigate the complexities of midlife, I've learned to approach each day with a sense of purpose, embracing the wisdom that pain often brings and the clarity that loss can sharpen.

The key to this journey is self-awareness, particularly in how I care for my body and soul. Holistic health is more than diet and exercise; it's about the harmonization of mind, body, and spirit. I've learned to nourish myself in ways that go beyond the physical; through meaningful relationships, through a spiritual practice that keeps me grounded, and through creating space for silence and reflection. These days, my focus is not on controlling the inevitable changes but on responding to them with patience and reverence.

There's also a new sense of responsibility as a single father. My daughter, with her innocence and resilience, reminds me daily that aging is not a solitary journey. In her eyes, I see the future and feel a renewed sense of purpose to lead by example; showing her how to navigate challenges, how to face setbacks with dignity, and how to love herself even when the world may not.

Aging, I've come to understand, is a dance with time. It's a gradual shedding of the layers we no longer need; old hurts, limiting beliefs, attachments to things that do not serve us. And in this shedding, I've found moments of peace. Life has slowed in ways I didn't expect, and the urgency of youth has softened into a steadier, quieter ambition.

While I continue to work hard—whether for my health, my career, or as a parent—I've begun to appreciate the importance of balance. Each morning, I strive to listen to what my body needs, to be more forgiving to myself when I fall short, and to practice gratitude for the moments of connection I share with my daughter, my family, and my close circle of friends.

The art of aging, for me, lies not in denying the process but in leaning into it with grace. It's about cultivating inner peace in the face of life's uncertainties, finding joy in simplicity, and embracing the profound beauty in the act of becoming. It's about loving deeply and living authentically, despite the scars and the struggles. My journey may have been fraught with hardship, but it has also been rich with learning, growth, and the unshakable belief that, even in the midst of it all, there is grace to be found.

–

An aging mentor, in fading grace,
With wisdom etched upon his face,
He speaks of life, of love, and pain,
As time slips by like autumn rain.

A student comes, week after week,
To listen close, to hear him speak,
Of work, and loss, and growing old,
Of tender truths both harsh and bold.

The body weakens, fails, decays,
Yet stronger still, the heart conveys,
That wealth is found in those we love,
In ties below and hopes above.

He teaches not to chase the gold,
But seek the warmth that hands can hold,
In fleeting time, find joy and grace,
For death, in life, we all must face.

Through parting words and final breath,
He shows the way to conquer death:
In giving love, we learn to live
And find in loss the strength to give.

—Sincerely, Boris

Most Sacred Of Responsibilities

As a father navigating life after divorce, I find myself contemplating my role and the legacy I leave for my daughter. In my journey, I've come to understand that within me lies an intrinsic value that extends beyond material provision or protection. It is the essence of fatherhood; a quiet strength, an inner authority that holds the potential to shape my daughter's understanding of the world, her future relationships, and her sense of self.

Fatherhood, I've learned, is not a measure of power, wealth, or societal success. Instead, it is the capacity to lead with humility, to serve with love, and to offer guidance through wisdom gained from experience. It is my responsibility to model integrity, resilience, and a balanced strength that embraces vulnerability. As I raise my daughter, I reflect deeply on the notion that a father's true power resides in his ability to inspire, to foster an environment of trust, and to be an anchor in moments of chaos.

The most profound lesson in my journey has been the realization that my role is not to be invulnerable but to allow my daughter to witness the full range of human emotion; courage in the face of adversity, calm in times of uncertainty, and grace in moments of failure. The authority I possess is not rooted in control but in the ability to create safety through consistency, to cultivate a space where my daughter feels seen, valued, and understood. I realize that in doing so, I teach her to trust herself, to recognize her worth, and to approach the world with both strength and compassion.

There is a sacred responsibility in fatherhood that transcends the ordinary. I have the ability to shape her perception of love, loyalty, and respect. The way I carry myself, the way I speak, listen, and act, will forever influence her expectations of the men she will one day encounter. This is not merely a passing influence but a lasting imprint. My presence, even in its quietest moments, speaks volumes.

In raising her, I am reminded that my greatest value lies not in grand gestures or words, but in the steadfastness of my character. The true impact of a father is in the small, consistent acts of devotion that accumulate over time. This legacy is one of presence, where I strive not for perfection but for authenticity, knowing that my daughter's well-being and strength are built upon the foundation I lay with intention, day by day.

What I have come to see is that my worth is not bound to what I have achieved but rather to how I have lived, how I have loved, and how I have fostered a space for her to thrive. The weight of this responsibility is profound, but so is the privilege of being entrusted with such influence. This, I believe, is the hidden value of being a man, a father, whose heart remains open to the lessons that life offers, so that I may, in turn, teach them to her.

—

Do we inherit, or do we create
The values that guide our family's fate?
Or do we craft, with hands and hearts, anew
A lineage of love, a broader view?

Values lived, yet seldom spoken,
In homes where the truth lies softly broken.
Could we not carve a stronger thread,
Where every soul, by these values, are fed?

When shared purpose lights the family flame,
Each person becomes more than just a name.
In words upheld and hearts aligned,
The legacy grows through time refined.

—Sincerely, Boris

Intersection

We met where the quiet honesty
of her profile drew me near.
A park bench held our stories
of loss, of love, of children's laughter,
and the delicate scars of past romance.

Time slipped through the cracks
of shared moments,
what seemed like minutes
stretching to an hour,
until she had to go.

At the corner where we first met,
she hugged me tightly,
a warmth I didn't know I needed.

I asked, she smiled,
and in the rush of the city,
our first kiss etched itself into the pavement,
marking the most beautiful intersection
Toronto will ever know.

—Sincerely, Boris

Pillow Talk

If our pillows could whisper,
would they guard our midnight confessions in quiet trust?
Or speak aloud the restless thoughts that stir beneath
closed lids?

Would the cool side, crisp and serene,
reflect calm restraint while the warm side,
worn with time, cradles our secrets with empathy?

Might they pass silent judgment on our habits,
Measuring devotion by how often we dress them in fresh
covers,
or feel exposed, vulnerable, without their shams?

Would they greet us gently at dawn, or lie mute,
Harboring the weight of unspoken fears
and dreams we've long buried?

Perhaps, in their silence, they offer solace;
A soft presence,
absorbing the burdens we cannot carry alone.

In the stillness of night,
they hold space for our heaviest thoughts;
Comforting us when the world falls quiet,
only they know the depth of our need for peace.

—Sincerely, Boris

Reclamation Of My Time and Energy

For much of my life, I found myself overextended, giving in to requests and demands that left me drained and resentful. My energy was siphoned away by others, leaving me little time or space to tend to my own needs.

In the pursuit of approval, or perhaps the avoidance of confrontation, I became a servant to the expectations of those around me. Yet I realized that this servitude was not borne out of obligation, but from my own inability to say "no"—a simple word, yet one that carries profound weight.

Learning to say "no" is, at its core, an act of self-preservation. It is not a rejection of others, but a reclamation of my time and energy. It is a statement of my boundaries, a way of asserting that my needs, desires, and well-being are just as valid as those of the people who ask for my help. The first step was recognizing that I am not responsible for meeting every expectation placed upon me. In fact, every time I said "yes" out of guilt or fear, I was betraying my own priorities, eroding my own autonomy.

The key to refusing others lies not in bluntness, but in clarity and conviction. To decline with grace, I needed to acknowledge that I am entitled to protect my time. By doing so, I discovered that I can offer more to the world when I am not constantly exhausted or overwhelmed. In reclaiming my ability to say "no", I opened up a reservoir of energy that could be redirected toward the things and people that matter most to me. It was not selfishness, but rather a conscious decision to steward my own resources wisely.

I also learned that guilt has no rightful place in this equation. The discomfort that arises from setting boundaries is temporary, and it pales in comparison to the long-term depletion caused by over-commitment. Others may not always understand, but their approval is not what defines my worth. There is immense power in standing firm, in recognizing that I cannot be everything to everyone. Saying "no" is an act of integrity to myself, and in turn, to those who truly depend on me.

By understanding the limits of my own capacity and cultivating the courage to enforce those limits, I now live with greater intention. Every "no" is a door that I close so that I may focus on the doors that truly lead to the life I want to create.

-

If you could hear the music once more,
Would you take my hand to the dance floor?
Would we recall each step we knew,
Or falter on the path we never grew?

Would I grasp at the chance
To share with you this last dance?

I shouldn't.
I couldn't.
I won't.

For this last dance
belongs to a heart
worthy of my embrace.

—Sincerely, Boris

The Greatest Gift Of My Life

Nearly five years ago, I made the difficult choice to leave a toxic and abusive marriage, a decision that came after realizing, through therapy, that the relationship had never truly served me. For years, I had cared for someone unable to care for themselves, losing parts of myself in the process. This choice took its toll mentally, physically, and financially, but it was necessary.

I remember telling myself, "I don't want to be here in five years, stuck in misery and pain". Now, as those five years draw to a close, I stand as proof of my promise to prioritize happiness; not just for my sake, but for that of my daughter, who means more to me than life itself. Despite enduring the trials of losing an eye, battling shingles, and surviving two brain aneurysms, I have emerged stronger, healthier, and more grounded than ever before.

My resilience is rooted in a deep determination for growth, and in the boundless strength my daughter gives me. She is my constant source of inspiration, my reminder of life's quiet wonders. Even though she is with me sixty percent of the time, her presence fills my world completely, showing me, through her compassion, empathy, and curiosity, how to embrace the beauty in every moment we share.

There was a time when she was taken from me while I worked relentlessly to create a stable life for her. I sacrificed time and sleep, and fought through my darkest hours, all with one aim: To build a future in which she could thrive. Each sacrifice, each sleepless night, was worth it to hold her close once again.

From the day she was born, I vowed to give her my best, to live up to my full potential as both her father and her friend. And I continue to fulfill that vow every day, cherishing every moment we spend together, knowing that our time is the most valuable thing I have. I take pride in watching her grow into a wonderfully creative soul, a lover of animals, nature, and crafting. She brings so much light into my life, and it's because of who she is that this journey as a single parent has felt lighter. She has made it easier; not through words, but through the way she simply exists, with a joyful spirit and quiet wisdom that has guided me as much as I have guided her.

There's an unspoken beauty in how we parent each other, even in moments when we're not aware of it. She has taught me patience, resilience, and the importance of seeing the world with wonder.

Together, we have made homes in new places, and each time, she has helped turn those spaces into sanctuaries, filled with love, laughter, and creativity. No matter where life takes us, I know that home will always be where we are together.

Being a single father has been the greatest gift of my life. It hasn't been easy, but it has been worth every challenge. Together, we've weathered the storms of separation and divorce, always finding our way back to each other, stronger. As I continue to watch her grow, I find myself in awe of the person she's becoming. And I will be here, by her side, in every step of her journey, just as she has unknowingly been there for me on mine.

—

Five years ago, I chose the way,
To leave the dark and find the day.
Through struggles deep and through strain,
I found my strength and peace from pain.

In those many years, nothing felt quite right,
And so I left behind the sleepless nights.
Through deep darkness and trials long,
I found my strength where I belong.

Her laughter lifts, her spirit shows,
In every moment, love still grows.
Her eyes reflect the world so true;
In her, I see all that we do.

We craft, we build, and shape our days
In nature's hands, where beauty stays.
She teaches me, though unaware,
In every smile, in every care.

Together, bound by love so tight,
We've turned our challenges to light.
In her, I find my greatest part;
My daughter, friend, my guiding heart.

—Sincerely, Boris

Inner Peace

Life is a collection of small moments, and within them, we find the essence of our existence. I've learned that comfort comes not from a place of constant joy but from an understanding that emotions, like the tides, ebb and flow. The key is acceptance; of sadness, of anxiety, of the inevitable uncertainties that life throws our way.

I now realize that healing often comes from unexpected sources, in acts of stillness, in the appreciation of simplicity. A cup of coffee, a walk in nature, reading under a big willow tree; all these carry the power to ground us when the world feels overwhelming. I've learned that it's okay to pause, to take a breath and acknowledge that being alive is itself a victory.

I've come to see that comparison is the thief of peace. Life's paths are varied, and each of us moves at our own pace. By detaching from expectations and external validation, I find a more authentic form of contentment. Resilience doesn't mean being unbreakable but understanding that we are allowed to be soft, allowed to lean on others when needed. There is strength in vulnerability, in admitting our fears and imperfections.

Ultimately, life isn't about grand gestures but about how we treat ourselves in the quieter moments. It's about nurturing our inner peace, about forgiving ourselves when we fall short, and about recognizing that we are enough as we are, in this moment. The journey toward peace is ongoing, but in each step, there is the possibility of grace.

—

In moments small, life shifts and flows
With highs and lows, as each day goes.
Embrace what comes, both joy and pain,
For nothing stays and change remains.

In simple acts, in quiet rest,
We find the calm that serves us best.
The cracks we bear, the flaws we show,
Are where the seeds of growth can flow.

We walk our path at our own speed,
No need to rush, no urge to lead.
In softness, strength, in stillness, care,
We're enough, just as we are, right here.

—Sincerely, Boris

Bids For Meaningful Connections

In my reflections on the architecture of human connection, I have come to understand that the foundation of any meaningful friendship is built upon a simple yet profound exchange; an offering of attention, a call for recognition, and the subtle dance of responsiveness. At the heart of every conversation, gesture, or shared silence lies the essential human need to feel seen and valued. It is in how we respond to these small, everyday moments that the bonds of friendship are either fortified or left to deteriorate.

The revelation that relationships thrive on the accumulation of "bids for connection" was deeply insightful. A bid may be as delicate as a smile or as direct as a request for advice. But what strikes me most is not the act itself but our response to it; whether we turn toward, turn away, or turn against. The strength of a friendship hinges on this moment of choice. Do I acknowledge the other, with all their complexities and needs, or do I withdraw into my own concerns, missing the chance for a deepened bond?

Turning toward someone means more than just a verbal response; it is the act of engaging with both heart and mind. It is being present not just physically but emotionally, signaling to the other that their presence matters. Friendships that thrive are borne out of this attentiveness. In contrast, turning away, even unintentionally, builds the invisible walls that distance souls, leaving unmet needs to fester.

Equally, I have found that conflict need not be feared but embraced as a natural part of any relationship's evolution. What matters is not the avoidance of disagreements but how we navigate them. When a disagreement arises, the true test of friendship is in how I express my concerns and how I receive theirs. Mutual respect and emotional attunement create the conditions where conflicts, far from being destructive, become the forge in which deeper understanding is shaped.

To foster this, I must hone my awareness of emotional cues, both within myself and in my friend. It is through the language of empathy that I can ensure my responses are grounded not merely in logic but in shared human experience. Compassion becomes the compass that guides us through even the stormiest of interactions, ensuring that, no matter the intensity of the moment, the bond remains intact.

It is the accumulation of small gestures, not grand acts, that determines the longevity and depth of a friendship.

-

What does it truly mean to call someone a friend? Is there an invisible gauge by which we measure the depths of connection, or is friendship a fluid construct, something we shape and redefine in our own way, moment by moment?

Is friendship borne from effortless communication, where words flow freely across the mundane and the profound? Do friends gather not only to share joy but to etch memories into the fabric of their lives? Is a friend the one who sits with us in silence, holding space for our darkest hours? Or are these gestures sometimes veiled in self-interest, wrapped in expectations we never consented to?

Is friendship a quiet agreement, a mutual understanding that transcends spoken terms? To be a friend, must one care deeply and love without restraint? Or are we merely passing ships, with one of us casting anchor while the other drifts away; still bound by the word "acquaintance", though our hearts tell different stories?

—Sincerely, Boris

Boundaries: A Declaration Of Self-Worth

Trust is a fragile thing, and I learned this through the bruises of past relationships. Boundaries were a concept I didn't recognize, let alone embrace. Throughout my childhood and young adult life, I hadn't seen trust protected by boundaries; instead, it felt conditional, something that could vanish the moment I made a mistake. Growing up in a home where my voice was often drowned out, where the lines between safety and fear blurred, I never learned that I had the right to set limits or protect my own space. As a child, I lived in an environment where mistakes felt unforgivable, with my needs and wants taking a backseat to keeping peace or avoiding conflict. That pattern followed me, undetected, into adulthood.

In my past marriage, trust was twisted into something transactional; I gave and gave, bending to make things work, hoping that in sacrificing my needs, I'd somehow earn security. But trust erodes quickly when there's no boundary to protect it, and by the time we reached the end, it was shattered, scattered in pieces I could barely recognize. Throughout the entire fourteen-year relationship with my ex-wife, I unknowingly carried the absence of boundaries with me. I tried to be everything I thought a husband and father should be, pouring every ounce of myself into a relationship that quietly depleted me, while she dictated our lives to the smallest detail, and often used them against me. My needs vanished under layers of compromise and concession. Over time, I realized I wasn't in love with her, but instead tethered by an obligation to uphold the image of a "good husband".

Boundaries felt selfish; they seemed like walls I wasn't allowed to build, even as my own well-being deteriorated. I had buried my true self beneath the weight of expectations and silent suffering. It took years to realize how damaging that was and how necessary it is to set limits that honor one's own dignity. After my divorce, I thought love alone would be enough to hold onto trust, but I soon saw how easily trust can be chipped away without boundaries to frame it. It taught me that when boundaries aren't respected, trust withers, leaving behind only doubt and regret. I realize now that boundaries are the silent guardians of trust. They keep it intact, protected from the misunderstandings that come when needs go unspoken. When I set boundaries, I'm not only safeguarding my well-being but also inviting others to respect my trust by respecting my limits. Learning to set boundaries has been, in many ways, a journey in rebuilding trust and that boundaries are an act of self-respect. They aren't barriers to keep people out, but lines that protect the best of who we are. I came to see that in order to show up as a healthy, present father, as a friend, as a partner, and as the person I strive to be, I need to safeguard my energy and my emotional space. Learning to set limits, to tell others where I end and they begin, has been a transformative act of reclaiming myself. I understand now that boundaries are not selfish; they are a declaration of self-worth. I had to understand that without boundaries, trust has no foundation; it's a vulnerable thing that requires support to stand on my own, and they're about creating a safe space where trust can grow slowly, steadily, and with integrity.

I have come to learn that when I honor my boundaries, I'm rebuilding the foundation of trust in myself. This trust is precious; it's the belief that I won't betray my own needs for someone else's comfort. They're a promise to myself that I will no longer give away pieces of my peace. And when others respect my boundaries, they earn something rare and valuable: A trust that, this time, feels solid enough to last. Through my experience, I've come to carry three powerful truths about boundaries. First, they are non-negotiable. For too long, I made my needs flexible, prioritizing others over myself. Now, boundaries allow me to define who I am, uncompromisingly. Second, they empower us to say "no" without guilt or apology. Each "no" is a way of saying "yes" to the life and relationships I deserve. And finally, boundaries are how we honor ourselves and teach others to do the same. They are my compass, helping me navigate life with dignity, pride, and authenticity.

This journey hasn't been easy. Breaking the patterns of a lifetime can feel like tearing down and rebuilding a house from its foundations. But I've learned that setting boundaries isn't about anger or resentment; it's about clarity, growth, and love; for myself, for my daughter, and for the relationships I wish to nurture moving forward.

—

Once there was a quiet garden,
filled with colors bright and wild.
It grew best when lines were honored;
a space for each root, each petal, each stem.
For a time, no borders stood,
and flowers tangled, starved for sun;
their colors dulled, their strength pulled thin,
as vines of one drained life from within.

So a gardener placed small stones around;
not walls, but paths for each to grow;
a space to bloom, freely and alone,
to lift their heads, to stretch and know.
In tending gently to each line,
the garden thrived, each flower freed,
and side-by-side, they grew in kind,
a beauty held by roots, not need.
Boundaries gave them life that way,
together, yet strong, every day.

—Sincerely, Boris

Healing Is Not Linear

I came to realize that healing from the emotional scars left by someone with narcissistic tendencies is not merely about reclaiming my life, but about rediscovering the essence of my being. It is a journey of disentangling myself from the web of manipulation, lies, and emotional control that I once mistook for love. This process revealed that the narcissist's need to dominate, devalue, and discard me was never a reflection of my worth, but rather a projection of their own inner void.

In this path of healing, I learned that understanding the narcissist's psyche, their need for constant validation and their deep-seated fear of vulnerability, was essential, not to excuse their behavior, but to reclaim my power. They thrive on chaos and thrive by distorting reality, making me question my own perceptions and feelings. However, the moment I began to trust my own intuition and emotions, the fog lifted. I saw that my boundaries were not weaknesses but strengths. Each boundary I set was an act of self-respect, an affirmation that I would no longer sacrifice my peace for the illusion of their love.

Healing was not linear, and often I found myself revisiting the pain, but with each step, I grew more resilient, more self-aware. I am learning to forgive; not to absolve them of their cruelty, but to release myself from the chains of resentment. The act of forgiveness is for my own liberation, freeing me to live without the darkness of the past dictating my unwritten future.

In reclaiming my autonomy, I cultivated self-love in ways I had forgotten. I nurtured my own emotional needs, found joy in simple things, and surrounded myself with people who genuinely saw me for who I was. My healing became an act of rebellion against the control once imposed upon me. In learning to love myself, I became whole again, unburdened by the weight of their narcissism, and I discovered the profound truth that my worth was never theirs to define.

—

I lost myself in her darkness;
The perception of love was tangled with deceit.
I break the chains of her illusion.
I began to reclaim the essence of who I am.

I forgive as an act of release;
not for her, but for my own liberation.
I let go of my past, my regrets, her control;
I began to see myself with more clarity,
realizing my worth had always been my own,
and never hers to abuse.

—Sincerely, Boris

The Quiet Confessions Of A Hopeless Romantic

I miss the simplicity of slow dancing, swaying with someone under dim lights or even no lights at all, just the music of the moment guiding us. I long for the quiet exchange of handwritten notes, folded corners, and scrawled words that felt more intimate than texting ever could. There's something irreplaceable about holding hands, feeling the pulse of another life interwoven with your own, a silent affirmation of connection.

I miss the affection; the casual, unspoken touches that say everything. The surprise of it all: An unexpected romantic gesture that brightened the day for no other reason than love. There's an almost sacred joy in taking care of someone when they're ill and not feeling themselves, the chance to nurture and be there in their vulnerability.

Cooking meals together, spending holidays together, planning a trip that revolves only around us, reading chapters to one another, carrying their things, buying flowers just because; these small rituals hold so much love in their simple execution. I miss sharing a stunning view with someone who feels the same way about the world, the silent communion that comes from recognizing beauty together.

Every love language matters in romance: The touch of a hand, the words that lift each other up, the thoughtful gifts, the unexpected surprises, the moments of service where we

care without being asked, and the time spent simply being.
They are all pieces of the puzzle that make romance whole,
that make it feel alive and present in every interaction.

—

I miss the fold of your notes,
handwritten, curved,
as if the words themselves
were meant only for us to read.

I miss the simple joy of your hand in mine,
our fingers woven tightly,
a quiet language spoken
through skin and pulse.

I miss the sudden warmth of affection,
unprompted touches that bloom
unexpectedly, like the harvest in your garden.

The element of surprise,
the way love shows up
in places we never thought to look.

I miss the kitchen conversations,
meals made with laughter
and slow dancing over a simmering pot.

And buying flowers, just because
a day felt brighter with them in your hands.
I miss the view from that hilltop,
how we lay there, silently drinking in the world's beauty
and found it mirrored in each other's eyes.

I miss the romance,
the essence of what made us whole,
the moments we froze in time,
just long enough to call them ours.

—Sincerely, Boris

Dorothy

Once in a rare while,
life graces us with a gift so pure,
it changes us forever;
leaving us better for the knowing,
a best friend.
From the first moment,
a quiet understanding,
as if we've walked alongside for lifetimes.
You zig-zag beside me,
through winding paths,
offering the kind of kindness
That feels like home.
You are the one
who dances with me
as if no one's watching,
who shares midnight feasts,
holds my hand through hardships,
shows up in the smallest moments
and the grandest.
Unwavering, constant,
unchanged by time or distance,
always bringing light, laughter,
and standing by my side
as I grow; becoming a husband, father, friend.

We've shared endless nights,
late confessions, plates of food,
trendy hairstyles, and laughter echoing through the years.
You were there through surgeries,
weddings, milestones,
more family than friend,
the other sibling I never knew I'd find.
In all the big moments, you are there.
And in the quiet ones, too.
The person I miss the second you leave,
already planning the next visit.
You've given me hope, love,
and a reminder of beauty in bonds
borne from shared history.

You are the one
I want to sing with at the top of our lungs,
to dance through the night,
to keep growing alongside.
You've filled my life with joy beyond words.
And I am proud of the woman,
mother, and friend you've become.
You are, and will always be,
my best friend.
Forever.

—Sincerely, Boris

Fluffy, My Dear Old Friend

We met when I was seven, in a hospital, in the small town I grew up in. My mother, pushing me in a wheelchair, the burn on my foot still fresh from a cup of boiling water. You sat waiting in the gift shop, calling out to me with a voice I'd never heard but somehow knew.

I reached for you, unaware that this first embrace would be the beginning of many, unaware that one day, I would hold you for the last time.

You returned to my hospital bed with me, staying close when my mother left for her night shift at the factory. Alone for the first time, I was surrounded by the echoes of patients' moans, machines' relentless beeping, footsteps that haunted the hallways. But there you were, steady in my arms, as I held you tightly, telling you I was glad you were there to keep me safe. You did, keeping your silent promise, as I woke the next morning with you in my grasp.

We shared a tray of breakfast, talked of crime-fighting turtles, and dreamed of adventures we'd have once I could leave this place. You became a part of me, so much so that when you vanished, it was as if a piece of me disappeared, too.

Many years had passed, and then, on my thirty-sixth birthday, my daughter handed me a bag. Inside, something felt familiar, warm, whispering my name. As I pulled you from the bag, there you were—my Fluffy, larger, whiter, but unmistakably you.

Now you rest on my bed once more, watching over as I sleep. My daughter whispers her dreams to you, as I once did. And I promise, I won't lose you again.

One day, when I am no longer here, you will live with her, offering the same comfort, watching over her sleep, as you did mine. Through you, we are connected across time.

—Sincerely, Boris

Releasing Resentment

For fourteen years, I carried the burden of a relationship that, in its quiet cruelty, convinced me that I was unworthy; a terrible husband, an inattentive father, a poor friend. Gaslit into self-doubt, I was made to believe that my flaws were responsible for the chaos. Yet, in truth, I was supporting a person who had every opportunity to stand on her own, but chose instead to lean into a narrative that kept her dependent and me in a cycle of sacrifice.

I was misled, tricked into doubting my loyalty as a friend, while I poured my best self into those I loved, calling them family. I was told I was failing as a father because I worked hard to provide, even though I always gave my daughter the fullness of my time and care, from reading bedtime stories to cooking meals and being present in the moments that truly mattered. Meanwhile, the person I shared my life with had next to no friends, no passions, no sense of fulfillment beyond the image she presented to the world.

The resentment I held onto was not born from singular events but from the accumulation of years spent sleeping on couches and floors, excluded from intimacy, and trapped in a performance of a marriage that lacked love. I poured time, money, and energy into preserving a façade that was never real. This false perception, of her, of us, was a thief that robbed me of my peace.

Letting go of this resentment does not mean that I dismiss the past, but it does mean that I reclaim the part of me that was buried beneath it. I must understand that control is often an illusion; the more I clung to the idea that I could change the outcome, the more I suffered. True freedom lies in accepting that life, and the people in it, are unpredictable. I cannot change who she was or how she treated me, but I can choose how I respond now.

Forgiveness, too, is not for her; it is a gift I give to myself. To hold onto anger, to nurture resentment, is to keep myself in chains long after the relationship has ended. I release that weight because my healing demands it, and my future deserves it.

As I look toward the future, I must embrace the present. The past, though painful, is no longer my prison; it is a foundation, a set of lessons that have fortified my resilience. My life now is a canvas I will fill with intention and authenticity, building upon the wisdom gained from the trials I've endured.

I have come to understand that letting go is not merely an act of forgetting, but a deliberate choice to free myself from the grip of the past, releasing the emotional weight that has bound me for too long. It requires an intimate confrontation with pain; not in the form of denial or suppression, but in a way that allows me to honor what has shaped me without letting it define the man I am becoming. The art of letting go, then, is not about erasing what has been, but about stepping into what is to come, with grace, peace, and open arms.

—

In a marriage built on illusions,
I lost pieces of myself,
Fighting to fit into a mold
That never reflected my truth.

Each sacrifice, a silent echo,
A yearning for connection
In a world of empty gestures.

Years passed, buried in doubt,
While destroying my spirit.
Until I knew it was time to leave,
To reclaim the life that I deserve.

With every step away from that past,
I peeled back the layers of shame,
Finding strength in my vulnerability,
And a voice that had long been hushed.

Now, I walk a path that is my own,
Embracing the unknown with open arms.
Each day is a chance to rebuild,
To honor the lessons learned,
And to celebrate the man I am destined to be.

No longer defined by what I lost,
I stand in the warmth of possibility
With a heart ready to heal
And a spirit renewed,
Ready to live fully
In the truth of my own story.

—Sincerely, Boris

Unwavering Support

Grief is not something one simply "gets over". It's a profound and transformative process that we learn to carry with us, reshaping it into wisdom and strength. Through my own experiences—surviving a traumatic childhood, navigating a toxic divorce, losing a best friend, and enduring health battles—I've come to realize that grief is best navigated with the support of others, not in isolation.

There are essential needs we must honor when mourning: Acknowledging the reality of loss, embracing the pain, and leaning on others to help carry the weight. Grief is not an experience to be rushed or solved, but rather a process of reconciliation; a deep acceptance that transforms us. Pain doesn't vanish, but with time and support, we learn to live alongside it. I've walked this path, understanding that grief becomes a part of us, woven into the fabric of who we are, reshaping our identity.

I've been incredibly fortunate to have a circle of friends and family whose love has carried me through the darkest moments. My older sister and twin brother, in particular, have been my constant companions in this journey. They were there during my childhood, when trauma was a silent presence. They stood by me through my divorce, when I questioned my worth as a husband and father. And they held me up through the grief of losing my best friend and the challenges of facing health issues that left me questioning my own mortality.

In my journey as a forty-one-year-old single father to my beautiful nine-year-old daughter, I've come to understand the profound depths of grief and the importance of embracing vulnerability. Grief is not merely an experience to endure but a courageous path toward healing and authenticity. It has taught me that acknowledging our pain allows us to connect more deeply with ourselves and others, paving the way for genuine mourning. Through my experiences in grieving past relationships, I've learned that vulnerability is a strength rather than a weakness. Recently, during a theater outing, my daughter witnessed my tears while watching *The Wild Robot*. On our walk home, she courageously asked me which parts of the movie had affected me the most. We paused on a bench, sharing our feelings and reflecting on the moments that sparked emotion within us. Together, we grieved for the old goose Longneck, honoring his courage and bravery for a few quiet moments.

This experience not only deepened our bond but also illustrated to her that expressing emotions is a natural and valuable part of life. In those moments, I realized that fostering an environment where feelings can be shared freely helps nurture resilience and empathy in her. By embracing our vulnerabilities, we honor our grief and create space for love, connection, and understanding, reminding ourselves that mourning is an integral part of our shared humanity. In navigating my own grief, I hope to guide her in finding the courage to authentically experience her emotions as she grows, assuring her that it's okay to feel deeply and openly in a world that often encourages the opposite.

What I've learned is that grief, in its purest form, is a communal experience. The presence of those who care for us is essential. It's in their company that I've found solace, in their compassion that I've discovered the strength to keep moving forward. The relationships that have endured through these hardships have been my lifeline, helping me process not only the pain of loss but also the profound sense of survival and rebirth that follows.

In my support group, I've found a space where vulnerability is met with understanding, where shared experiences foster healing. These connections have reminded me that we are not meant to bear the weight of our grief alone. My siblings' generosity and my friends' loyalty have allowed me to reshape my pain into something meaningful. Through them, I've found the courage to keep walking this path, not in spite of the losses I've faced, but because of the love that surrounds me.

Grief may be inevitable, but it is not insurmountable. With time, with patience, and with the unwavering support of those who care for us, we can reconcile our losses and create a new understanding of who we are. In the end, it's the love we receive that helps us carry the grief; and in that love, we find the strength to continue.

—

It's as if you've spent a lifetime in pursuit, tirelessly honing your craft, only to meet the moment you've long awaited, and falter. In that instant, the prize you held so tightly slips through your fingers, drifting out of reach, lost forever.

Every step, every sacrifice, has led you here, only for the dream you chased so relentlessly to dissolve before your eyes. The weight of expectation presses down, and the failure burns deep, rending your heart in waves, relentless in its ache.

But at the end, where defeat seemed inevitable, something unexpected awaits. There, beyond the finish line, stand the ones you love most; cheering, smiling, their eyes bright with pride. Their applause whispers a truth louder than your loss: That second place is but a number. In their eyes, you have always been, and will always be, their champion.

—Sincerely, Boris

Endless Loop

Every time I see you, it's the first time again;
like déjà vu rewritten in softer shades,
and I fall, surrendering as though I'd never known
the way you can both heal and haunt me.
I step into this circle, unbroken and sweet,
each glance a welcome wound, a familiar ache,
as if my heart has never learned
the shape of letting go.
I've tried to leave,
to walk ahead or fold back in,
but I'm tethered to the memory of you,
an orbit I can't escape,
falling faster each time I rise.
I want to remember you less, but find myself
lingering in every echo of your name,
bound to relive each look, each touch;
this time loop of you, pulling me deeper,
until it's all I know,
and all I want to leave behind.

—Sincerely Boris

For Safekeeping

If you were an email,
I'd mark you with stars,
tuck you away in a quiet corner,
where your words would be safe
for keeping.

If you were a song,
I'd let your melody spill through me,
again and again,
holding each note in a playlist
for keeping.

If you were a quote,
I'd trace your meaning, line by line,
etch you softly in the pages of my heart
for keeping.

If you were a drink,
I'd savor each drop slowly,
letting the taste linger on my lips
for keeping.

If you were a breath of fresh air,
I'd inhale you gently,
fill my lungs with your essence
for keeping.

If you were a photograph,
I'd gaze into your stillness,
press you into the folds of memory
for keeping.

If you were a clay pot,
I'd plant beauty in your depths,
let you bask in sunlight's warmth
for keeping.

If you were mine,
I'd cradle your soul tenderly,
hold you through the ages of time
for safekeeping.

—Sincerely, Boris

Depth Of My Intimacy

There was a time when I believed that intimacy was something instinctual, a force that either existed between two people or didn't. But over time, I came to understand that intimacy is not simply a given; it is something that must be nurtured through honest and vulnerable conversations, each revealing the heart of what we need, fear, and desire.

I learned that the foundation of connection lies in acknowledging my deepest longings; those desires that go beyond physicality. It required me to unravel the layers of what I want, to express the complexities of attraction, and to embrace the discomfort of speaking my truth. Only by facing these unspoken needs could I truly invite another into the depth of my intimacy.

I also had to confront the tension between pleasure and discomfort. There's an art in balancing these two forces, in recognizing that not every touch, every moment, will be perfect. It became clear to me that boundaries are essential, that knowing when to say "yes" and when to say "no" is as much a part of intimacy as the act of coming together. The body speaks in these moments, revealing both joy and hesitation, and I had to learn to listen.

Trust, I realized, is the heartbeat of connection. It is not enough to want intimacy; it must be built on a foundation where vulnerability can flourish. This is a trust that goes beyond words; it requires action, consistency, and the courage to be fully seen. In moments of doubt, I had to open myself further, revealing my flaws and insecurities, knowing that trust isn't something to be passively given but actively cultivated.

And then there's the rhythm of how we communicate; the delicate balance of speaking and listening. I found that the most profound conversations are often those that leave space for silence, for reflection. Patience became my ally, as I learned that empathy in communication creates a shared experience, one that allows both of us to feel understood without the need for constant resolution.

But perhaps the most transformative realization was understanding that intimacy is not static. It evolves, just as we do. My body, my desires, and the way I seek connection have changed over time, and I've come to accept this as part of the journey. Rather than clinging to past versions of ourselves, I found a certain grace in adapting, in continually exploring new ways to nurture both trust and pleasure.

In the end, these realizations became more than lessons. They became a practice; an ongoing commitment to creating space for intimacy that is as rich emotionally as it is physically. It's a space where love deepens, where empathy and passion intertwine, and where both partners are given the freedom to grow alongside each other.

—

It's in the breath between words,
A place where we meet,
Beyond the edge of touch,
Where skin is not a barrier, but a bridge.

It's in the slow unraveling of the heart,
Our truest selves,
Waiting to be seen,
waiting to be held.

Intimacy is the courage to stay,
Where bodies bend,
Not just for the warmth of another,
But for the release of what we carry alone.

The eyes that undress what words cannot,
The trust that grows
Not from promises spoken,
But from the weight of presence of being whole.

Where love is not just felt
But understood
In the way we share our breath,
Our silence,
Our fears,
And our fire.

—Sincerely, Boris

Between Body, Mind and Soul

Intimacy had long become a delicate subject for me, a source of frustration and insecurity, cultivated over years of living in a sexless marriage devoid of intimacy. For almost twelve years, I found myself in a space where physical connection with my ex-wife felt distant, out of reach, and complicated by a persistent silence around the topic. Over time, the absence of conversation about sex, its desires, its needs, or its nuances, began to shape my own relationship with it; it became something uncomfortable, something I didn't know how to approach, even with myself.

Throughout those twelve years of that relationship, there was a constant undercurrent of frustration and loneliness that I tried to manage on my own. But often, the silence within my failed marriage grew too heavy, and I turned to my closest friends for advice, for solace, for some way to understand the void. It became a recurring conversation; seeking their guidance on how to navigate the emotional isolation, how to make sense of a relationship that felt disconnected and barren in one of its most essential dimensions. I would disclose my frustration, confide my fears, and ask for advice, yet the answers never seemed clear, and the weight of it all only deepened.

Despite the vulnerability I shared with them, and despite their best attempts to offer counsel, the core issue remained; there was a gap in my relationship that couldn't be bridged by external advice alone. Friends could empathize, they could validate my feelings, but they couldn't untangle the knot of silence that existed between me and my partner. I would often return from those conversations feeling a mix of relief and sadness; relief from sharing my burden, but sadness in knowing that the answer still lay in a conversation that I wasn't having with the one person I needed to speak to the most, which was always met with passive aggression.

Over time, I came to understand that no amount of external advice could fix what was missing internally. It was only when I learned how to confront the topic of intimacy directly, with openness and honesty, that I began to see a path forward. The discomfort I had once felt, the awkwardness, the insecurity, began to dissolve as I realized that these conversations weren't about blaming or fixing the past, but about creating a future for myself that allowed for intimacy and connection.

The years of loneliness, the countless conversations with friends, had all pointed toward one fundamental truth: that the strength of any intimate relationship lies in the ability to communicate openly about the things that are most difficult. And in my case, intimacy had become a symbol of that difficulty, a space of silence that I needed to break open in order to reclaim a part of myself.

What I came to understand is that, like any other aspect of a partnership, intimacy requires communication. It is more than just the physical act; it is emotional, mental, and spiritual, a space of vulnerability that cannot thrive in silence. I learned to see intimacy as an essential form of expression, not merely of desire, but of love, connection, and shared humanity. Yet, in the absence of conversations, it had been reduced to a hollow echo of what it could be, leaving me unsure of how to navigate my own needs and desires.

The wisdom I uncovered throughout the recent years was that to heal this space, to revive intimacy, one must first confront the silence. I needed to learn how to approach the topic, not with trepidation, but with clarity and openness, and without the shame of my sexless marriage when meeting new romantic partners. It became clear that creating a foundation of trust required speaking about sex; not as an obligation, not as something to fix, but as something to explore, to grow into together, with curiosity and patience. In many ways, these conversations became a way to reclaim a part of myself, to address the years of neglect and the emotional weight that had settled in its place. Today, I am proud to be able to communicate openly about this fractured part of my failed marriage.

There is no one formula for addressing these conversations, but there is power in simply starting. It helped me understand that vulnerability in talking about intimacy is not a weakness but a strength; an invitation to intimacy that extends far beyond the physical. I learned that by facing the discomfort, I could redefine what intimacy meant to me, turning it from a source of insecurity into a space of shared discovery. It became less about performance or meeting expectations and more about connection, between body, mind, and soul.

In time, I grew more comfortable with my desires, with voicing them, and in hearing the desires of future romantic partners. The fear that had once paralyzed me slowly gave way to a newfound confidence; not only in my ability to give and receive love, but in my capacity to be honest about what I needed. It is a continuous journey, but now I understand that approaching intimacy with openness, respect, and communication is key to creating a deeper, more fulfilling connection.

—Sincerely, Boris

Ceaseless Questioning

For as long as I can remember, my mind has been a vast and restless sea, where thoughts rise and fall in waves, sometimes calm, other times stormy and relentless. I have always carried within me the tendency to overthink, to analyze, dissect, and replay events in an endless mental cycle, trying to extract meaning or anticipate what lies ahead. Recognizing this as an essential part of who I am, I have nonetheless devoted myself to learning how to temper its weight.

In time, I have found that the journey to inner stillness begins with presence: The realization that true peace resides solely in the passing moment, a truth both elemental and profound. Rather than letting the mind pull me into hypothetical futures or past regrets, there is a lesson to savor the stillness found in today, a simplicity that both shelters and liberates me. This self-discipline of anchoring myself to the present frees me from the prison of my own thoughts—a notion that I, as a lifelong seeker of self-betterment, find humbling—and frees me from the confines of a mind otherwise driven toward ceaseless questioning.

Through this pursuit, I have also learned how to take a gentler approach toward myself. I no longer try to control or reshape every thought; instead, I watch them as they arise, holding them in compassion, allowing each one to pass, like clouds drifting through an open sky. In a life marked by losses, heartbreaks, and personal challenges,

I've learned that my thoughts are neither adversaries nor burdens, merely travelers in my mind's landscape, appearing and departing in their own time.

Another insight is the understanding that not all problems demand an immediate solution. This is one I've wrestled with deeply, as I tend to seek resolution and order. But in realizing that some answers reveal themselves in time, I've found an unexpected strength in patience. Accepting uncertainty, even discomfort, has been liberating, a quiet revolution of spirit, inviting me to embrace life's unknowns.

In the end, I see that the path to peace is unending, an ongoing practice of becoming. Each day, I am reminded that I am not my thoughts but the quiet awareness beneath them, a space of stillness untouched by any turmoil. In accepting this, I've uncovered a quiet strength in patience, a willingness to reside within life's uncertainties and to welcome even discomfort as part of the whole. Through all my efforts, I am learning to hold onto this wisdom, a steadying hand in a world that never stops churning.

—

I sit and spin the web of "why"
Tugging threads that cloud my mind,
Of could-have-beens and might-have-seens,
Where echoes haunt the in-betweens.

I parse each word, rewind each breath,
Reframe the scene of an endless quest.
But truth slips by like morning mist,
Lost in the maze, my mind has kissed.

And still, I loop around again,
Bound to a past that won't unbend.

—Sincerely, Boris

Listen Closely

Listening, truly hearing, and validating others are more than just transactional actions; they are pathways to deeper connection and understanding. As I navigate relationships in my life, be it as a brother, father, friend, or romantic partner, I recognize the invisible barriers that often obstruct meaningful communication. These barriers are rooted in assumptions, judgments, or emotional distractions that distance us from one another.

With my parents, the distance is palpable. It's not simply a physical separation but an emotional one, built over years of unmet expectations and miscommunications. Listening, I've learned, involves more than just being present; it's about silencing my inner critic and fears long enough to truly hear them, to understand their perspectives without immediately reacting or defending. This is where the challenge lies: How do I open myself to a history that's been difficult without letting it consume me?

My siblings have always been my emotional anchors. Here, I've discovered the importance of validation, not just through words, but through actions and shared experiences. In these relationships, we've built a foundation of trust, and I've realized that validating their experiences means offering empathy without judgment, even when I don't fully understand. In return, I've felt their unwavering support through the darkest moments of my life.

With my daughter, as a single father, listening has taken on new meaning. She looks to me not just for answers, but for guidance through her emotions, her thoughts, and her evolving sense of the world. Hearing her is about allowing her the space to express herself without imposing my own fears or expectations. It's about creating an environment where she feels safe and valued, knowing that her thoughts matter, that her voice is important. I've found that validating her as she grows is my way of not only being her father but also being her ally in life.

Friends and romantic partners have presented their own challenges. In my past relationships, I've often found myself either shutting down or misinterpreting, letting misunderstandings brew into distance. What I've learned is that to truly connect with those I care for, I need to offer them more than just words; I need to offer presence, patience, and the willingness to acknowledge their emotional realities without diminishing them. It's an ongoing process of learning to hold space for others while also being vulnerable enough to let them hold space for me.

Through all these roles, I've come to understand that listening, hearing, and validating are not just tools for better relationships; they are acts of love and generosity. When I strip away my ego and the defenses I've built over years of pain and trauma, I see that these practices are what allow me to bridge the gaps that have formed in my life, from my childhood through to the present. They are, ultimately, how I can transform the relationships that matter most to me, starting with myself.

—

There's a secret to listening, a delicate art,
Where ears become wings and minds become hearts.
It's not just the words that float through the air,
But the spaces between, the moments we share.

It's catching the whispers that never take flight,
The thoughts in the corners, the ones out of sight.
Like fireflies dancing in soft twilight skies,
It's hearing the things that aren't said with your eyes.

A laugh that feels tired, a smile that's unsure,
A pause that says "listen", though nothing is pure.
It's the music of presence, a soft-spoken tune,
That fills up the room like a warm afternoon.

To listen, my friend, is an act of sweet grace,
A gift without ribbons, no bow to replace.
For love isn't grand when you shout from above;
It's the quiet "I hear you" that whispers of love.

—Sincerely, Boris

Witch Hunt

They gathered under moonlight's veil,
Lovers hidden, soft, and frail.
They dared to love, to heal, to be;
Marked as evil, wild, and free.
Queer loving hands and whispered spells,
They were cast as wicked, cursed to hells.
Bound in fire, bruised by blame,
Yet in secret, they kept their flame.
Witches walked where shadows crept,
While silent fears and hatreds slept.
Outcast hearts, they forged their way;
Through darkness, hate, and fiery fray.
Still, their spirits haunt the skies,
Their courage born where danger lies.
The world remembers love's brave cost,
And all they were, though deemed as lost.
Yes, they loved, no sin, no shame;
Women to women, men the same.
True to heart and soul's design,
Their love, power, old, divine.

—Sincerely, Boris

A Haiku: The Super Moon

Tonight's super moon
shines brighter than The Harvest;
Welcome, The Hunter.

—Sincerely, Boris

Muted

It has never been clearer:
This silence is mine to wield,
A shield against all transmissions,
A promise I made to guard my heart,
Even if it meant losing you.

To escape the endless circles,
And quiet the mind's relentless loops,
I vowed to retreat into silence.
This vow is not just for me,
But for those who inhabit the words
I've longed to speak,

Words I have meticulously crafted,
But will never release into the air.
For I no longer need the noise
To anchor my peace.
I refuse to let my words define me,
To sabotage my healing.

Instead, I rest in silence,
Where my truth can breathe, unbruised.
I will stay quiet, and distant;
For in this silence, I have found my strength.
Louder now than ever before,
I grow and protect what awaits me
In the spaces life has yet to fill.

—Sincerely, Boris

Resilient Women

To my sister, you have been a constant source of support and inspiration. You took on the role of a caretaker when we were still children ourselves, guiding us through challenges that were far beyond what anyone your age should have faced. It astonishes me that you are only a year and a half older than I am; I have always seen you as a pillar of strength and wisdom. Your sacrifices, often unnoticed, were made to help our parents navigate their new life, and your resilience has shaped who I am today. You have shown what it means to be nurturing, patient, and compassionate, qualities I aspire to instill in my own daughter. I honor you for the strength and values you have passed on to me and to our brother.

To my sister-in-law, the little sister I never had, I feel fortunate to have you in my life. Your love and loyalty to my brother are a reflection of the strong bond we share. You truly embody what it means to be a family member. The comfort and joy you bring to him speak volumes about the remarkable woman you are. Over the years, I have admired your growth and dedication to your craft, which continually inspires me. Your creativity and commitment to building a life filled with love and purpose are qualities I deeply respect. My daughter looks up to you, and it's easy to see why; you set a wonderful example for her. I honor you through my appreciation of your generosity and your determination to excel.

To my mother, thank you for doing your best with what you had. I know it wasn't easy moving to a new country with little to offer, and you aspired to give us more than you received. Our relationship had its challenges; we often struggled to communicate our feelings, but I recognize the sacrifices you made for our family. Your resilience and work ethic taught me the value of perseverance. Despite our limited means, you always found a way to share what little you had, and those small gestures have meant everything to me. I honor you by working hard and being grateful for what I have, rather than focusing on what I lack.

To my daughter, you are the center of my world. From the moment I first saw you, my perspective on life shifted. You have shown me the kind of father I aspire to be; protective, supportive, and nurturing. Your kindness, curiosity, and empathy remind me of what truly matters in life. I hope you always hold on to these qualities as you grow. You inspire me daily to strive for personal growth and to become the best version of myself. Each day spent together is a gift, and I am grateful to be your father. I honor you by making choices that lead to a healthy and hopeful future, always encouraging you to dream big and pursue your passions. You will always be my daughter, and I will always be here to support you.

—

Strength in the silence, fierce hearts that ignite,
With patience and wisdom, they claim their birthright.
Determined and bold, with compassion that's deep,
In the bonds of sisterhood, their spirits leap.

They rise unyielding, with voices that soar,
Breaking the barriers, demanding much more.
With kindness and courage, they stand side-by-side,
United in purpose, their spirits our guide.

In their grace and their grit, they find our own might;
Together they flourish, igniting the light.

—Sincerely, Boris

Nurturing Her Curiosity

As a father, I have been entrusted with life's most precious gift: A love without condition, the privilege to nurture and guide a soul as it blooms into something extraordinary. These fleeting moments are equal parts thrilling and terrifying, each one a gem, etched in the depths of memory like the most sacred of recordings. They capture growth, stumbles, triumphs, and milestones, each step shaping our daughters into resilient, independent women. Women who lift one another, unite in strength, and rebuild a world where they lead with grace and wisdom.

From the moment I first gazed upon my daughter, her eyes met mine with an unspoken question, a silent wonder. She asked a thousand things, yet I could only return the same gaze, full of awe. How astonishing she was; this new life, cradled in my arms, an extension of myself. For every question she had, a hundred more unfolded in my heart. Who will she become? What will her voice carry? How will our love manifest as she grows?

As the years have passed, she has answered each question, both in subtle, fleeting moments—laughter, tears, resilience, dance—and through our conversations, at the dinner table, on swing sets, on our long walks, and in the quiet calm of bedtime.

With each answer, new questions emerge, and so we trade curiosity, passing it back and forth like our own secret language. What kind of friend will she be? What passions will drive her? What books will she like to read? What will our bond mean to her as time moves forward?

She has never hesitated to ask the hard questions; about my failed marriage, my surgeries, my relationships, my fears. And in asking, she would often offer the answers herself. In doing so, she has shown me the depth of her growth, the person I have always wondered who she would become.

I will never cease to nurture and encourage her curiosity, nor will I ever stop embracing the questions she asks. And though I may never stop wondering: What will she do when I am no longer here? Who will be there to care for her? How will she remember me? I know this: Her curiosity will lead her, as it has always led me.

Our mission is to foster their intellectual curiosity, teach them the weight of choices, and empower them to know their worth. We show them love firsthand, cultivate their growth, teach them the value of gratitude, and then, when the time comes, we set them free to soar.

-

Don't clear every hurdle in their way
or hover close above.
They'll never find their own way
if we mistake fear for love.

It's not our place to smooth their path,
or "snowplow" and "helicopter" away each test.
But to stand beside them and watch them grow,
as they learn to do their very best.

We raise them not for ease, but good,
with hearts both kind and strong.
For in each challenge they will grow
and learn where they belong.

Let's guide our children, but let them lead,
and trust them as they make mistakes.
For they must pave a lane for themselves,
to be able to fix what they break.

—Sincerely, Boris

Today, I Release You

Today, I took down photos of us, images that once captured your smile, our laughter, our closeness, but now reflect only the distance between who we were and who we've become.

Today, I tucked away your gifts, the books you pressed into my hands and read out loudly in my mind, the small tokens of affection that once whispered of forever. Each one a reminder of a love that has since withered, no longer nourished by our presence.

Today, I folded your favorite sweaters, still faintly carrying the scent of you, a scent that once filled my world with comfort, but now lingers like a ghost of what was. The sweaters, once wrapped around you like comfort, now drape in cold silence, and so I tuck them away, symbols of a warmth long gone.

Today, I put away the image of the way your hair caught the morning light. I let go of the thoughts of the lines on your face, the ones I once traced with love, now rest in the quiet spaces of my memory.

Today, I said goodbye to how your dog curled up on the couch, the silent witness to our long conversations. Those deep, winding exchanges where we unraveled the universe and found solace in each other's thoughts are now sealed away with the rest.

Today, I pressed these memories to the edges of my heart, where they once brought me joy, but now they stir only hollow echoes of emotions that have long since faded.

In this act of release, I shed the weight of misplaced optimism, the futile questions that kept us tethered to a love story that no longer holds true.

Today, I am learning to let go of the version of us I once cherished, surrendering the past that occupies the space where new beginnings must take root. By clearing this path, I open myself—emotionally, spiritually—to what may come, to what I am now ready to receive.

Tomorrow, I will greet the future with open arms, free from what was, ready to embrace what could be. But for now, I create space for possibility, for love, for myself.

–

This may be hard to hear, or not at all,
The space between us, the echo of the fall,
A silence stretching further with each day,
A tether worn thin, now slipping away.

Whatever this is, it cannot remain—
A friendship, or the ghost of what became.
We've drifted, strangers in a distant land,
Clinging to the ashes of what we once planned.

No longer do I wish to play this part,
Forcing something absent from the start.
Let the silence rest where words can't go;
Let peace follow where the winds now blow.

Our efforts mirrored the love we had,
Yet in their absence, I can't be sad.
Desire fades like whispers in the dark,
And leaves us both unanchored, worlds apart.

This was not easy, and never could be,
But the truth is the light that finally set me free.
No response is needed, no plea for more,
Only honesty to settle this inner war.

I felt us working toward this end,
Each step unspoken, unable to mend.
But now the courage has found its voice,
And with it comes the freedom of choice.

You were a great friend once, this is true,
And I hope I was the same for you.
Let's hold the beauty of what we were,
Not the distance we've become, a distant blur.

So farewell, my friend, as we part ways,
May your life be full of brighter days.
Let time and space gently define
The moments when our hearts aligned.

Goodbye, dear friend, and know this, too,
I'll remember the best of what was me and you.

—Sincerely, Boris

Home Is Where The Heart Is

Have you ever tried to describe what love feels like? To me, everything points to home. Not as a place of living, but a feeling you get when something is so familiar; something you have an immediate meaningful connection to. I feel like this with my daughter, with my siblings, with my closest friends; and this came to me as I was reflecting on a past relationship, when asking myself what it was like to be with this person. Everything pointed to that feeling of being home no matter where we were. It was safe, warm, comfortable, and sometimes uncomfortable. So maybe it's that simple. Love feels like home. And the goal is to build a neighborhood.

—

As I stand at the water's edge, where the sea meets the sky,
Waves of emotion crash, blurring the line between past and present.

Yet through the fog, your light shines, a beacon of hope;
Guiding me, steady, through the storm, revealing a path I could not see.

In the end, it wasn't you at the horizon,
It was me, always me, waiting to be found.
But it was your strength, your hope, that carried me through the tide.

Now, as our journey fades with the setting sun, I let go;
Thank you, old friend, for steering me home when I was
lost at sea.

So long, and farewell.

—Sincerely, Boris

Currency Of Time

How many of us move through life, unknowingly drawing our final breath, spending our last hour with someone we believe we will see next week, sharing our final meal with someone we hold dear, watching our last film, listening to our final song, or reading the last page of another's story?

One truth about life, seldom spoken, is that with every day we live, we are also dying. From the moment we are born, we inch closer to death. We pass through life, accumulating loved ones, possessions, and experiences—but to what end?

If we are all merely running toward the inevitable, then let us accumulate all that brings us joy. Be remembered as a collector of everything and everyone you love. And most importantly, tell them how you feel, before the last days arrive and your chance slips away.

-

From our first breath, the seconds slip,
Spent in a currency we scarcely grip.
We waste it on what's broken, worn,
While neglecting the beauty newly born.

Too often, we fixate, we stall,
Forgetting to build, to love, to call;
Moments that ripple, memories that bind,
Treasures more lasting than what we leave behind.

Time, the one gift we all possess,
Dwindles down with each caress.
And when we exhale our final sigh,
We'll wish we'd spent it not asking why,

But shaping moments that outlast death;
For time, not life, is our final breath.

—Sincerely, Boris

Power Of Touch

I've always craved touch, though it wasn't always present in my life. Growing up in a home devoid of affection, I learned to navigate the world without the comfort of a gentle hand or a warm embrace. It left me longing for something unspoken, a yearning for connection that went deeper than words could provide. For years, that craving remained unmet, especially during my fourteen-year relationship with my ex-wife, where intimacy was sparse, and the absence of touch became a painful reminder of the emotional distance between us.

Touch, as I've come to understand, is not just physical. It's a language of its own, a way to communicate safety, belonging, and love. In every handshake, hug, or brush of the skin, there's an exchange of something more; a silent understanding, a bond forged. It's why I've always gravitated towards expressing love with hugs, with high-fives, or just by being close to those I care about. These moments of contact transcend the surface and speak to a deeper need for connection.

The joy of nurturing relationships with past girlfriends, where touch became a bridge between hearts, showed me the power of physical affection. There was something profoundly healing in holding hands, feeling the warmth of another's skin, or embracing without the need for words. It's the simplest of actions, yet it grounds us, makes us feel seen and understood in ways no other form of communication can.

And then there's my daughter, the living embodiment of the love I never received as a child but have always sought to give. Holding her in my arms, carrying her on my back or shoulders, I've come to realize that the act of touch between a parent and child is as much about protection as it is about love. It is a reminder that I am here, that I am present in a way I once wished someone had been for me.

Through these experiences, I've come to understand that touch is not just a biological need but a profound emotional one. It shapes who we are, how we connect with others, and ultimately, how we find peace within ourselves. It's a reminder that we are, at our core, creatures of connection, yearning to be held, touched, and loved—whether through the grasp of a hand, the warmth of a hug, or the simple presence of another.

—

The gentle art of giving and receiving,
in every caress, every warm embrace,
connections reaffirmed, and doubts are eased.

Through your touch, I discover my truth,
A silent language speaking to both me and you,
Our words unspoken yet profoundly understood,
Where trust and safety are love are cured.

Bound by the tender essence of intimacy,
In this sacred space, love's essence is revealed,
A testament to the power of touch, unconfined;
The power to heal, deep and sincere.

—Sincerely, Boris

Foundations

The day unfolds with a heart steeped in gratitude, stirred awake by morning meditation. The afternoon finds me beneath a willow's gentle sway, a book cradled in my hands, warmth rising from a mug beside me. As night whispers its arrival, my thoughts spill onto paper, paired with a quiet indulgence. Each moment carries the weight of intention, weaving a rhythm of mindfulness, stillness, and creativity. It's a ritual that nourishes my spirit, cultivating inner peace, self-discovery, and inspiration in its delicate balance.

–

Through meditation, we sit with what arises,
learning to stay present with our thoughts,
to breathe into the pain of our experiences.

No longer fleeing discomfort,
we meet our fears with open arms,
letting them speak, letting them go quietly.

The thoughts, the worries, the pain;
all given the mental space to exist,
but no longer bound by our need for control.

We hold them lightly,
and as we loosen our grip,
they all begin to drift away.

In this stillness, our healing begins,
slow and unfolding,
a lifelong journey until we are reborn.

We embrace the unknown,
finding peace in the spaces in between;
holding on and letting go.

—Sincerely, Boris

Quarter of an Hour

In the first quiet stir of morning light,
I make a solemn promise to myself,
Fifteen minutes of gratitude, a gift,
To let yesterday's burdens dissolve away,
And welcome the new day, clean and soft.

The next quarter of the hour, I move with purpose;
Making my bed, cracking eggs, waiting as the toast crisps.
I vow not to rush the ritual,
But to savor the warmth of the day's first sip,
Knowing this moment is mine to hold.

In the next space of time, my eyelids fall,
And in the stillness, I allow my mind to rest.
I gift myself the kindness of breath,
A meditation on silence, on peace,
Each breath is a tender reminder to simply be.

The final fifteen I devote to my thoughts,
Unfolding visions, dreams, and gratitude,
Mapping the horizon of what might be,
As I rise with intention
To greet my day and its untold potential.

—Sincerely, Boris

Compassion: A Way Of Being

In my journey toward embracing compassion as a way of being, I've come to understand that the path to selflessness is not about denying myself, but rather expanding my sense of self to include the wellbeing of others. Every moment presents an opportunity to awaken the heart, to lean into discomfort rather than avoid it, and to cultivate a deep empathy that transcends personal interests.

I've learned that the practice of compassion involves recognizing the suffering in the world without becoming overwhelmed by it. It's about training the mind to meet challenges with patience and openness, seeing others' pain as a reflection of our shared human condition. When I make a commitment to serve others, I am not striving for perfection but rather accepting my own imperfections as part of the learning process.

Through mindful awareness, I realize that my own difficulties and struggles are a gateway to greater understanding and connection. By confronting fear and vulnerability, I begin to soften my heart, not just toward others but toward myself. Compassionate action is not grand gestures but small, consistent choices to live with kindness, equanimity, and courage. It is a practice of being present, attentive, and fully engaged with life as it unfolds.

The key teaching is that real transformation comes not from external achievements or recognition but from the inner work of shifting from self-centeredness to a broader, more inclusive perspective. True freedom arises when I let go of the need to protect my ego and embrace the interconnectedness of all beings, recognizing that my happiness is inextricably tied to the happiness of others.

—

Compassion is seeing what hurts
and staying close anyway.
It's the hand that helps you up
without asking for thanks.

It doesn't turn away
when things get hard,
and it doesn't fix,
just shows up.

It's the quiet presence
that makes room for pain,
a choice to stand with someone
even when you can't solve a thing.

Compassion is simply being there;
eyes open, heart open,
willing to share the weight
for as long as it takes.

—Sincerely, Boris

Truth, Reconciliation, And What It Means
To Canadian

Growing up as an immigrant from São Paulo, Brazil, I was eager to assimilate into what I thought of as the quintessential Canadian life: Road hockey, the Toronto Blue Jays, the peaceful multiculturalism I heard so much about. My early years in Canada were shaped by the simple desire to belong, to be seen as a regular Canadian kid. I was proud to be here, in what I viewed as a land of opportunity and kindness. But as I grew older, so did my understanding of this country's complicated history, one that runs deeper than the friendly stereotypes I had once embraced.

It took time to see that this land I was so eager to call home had a much darker past, particularly in its relationship with Indigenous communities. There's a truth to this country's story that unsettled me as I learned more about the legacy of colonization, residential schools, and the continued struggles of Indigenous peoples. At first, it was hard to reconcile these facts with the Canada I thought I knew: A nation that promised fairness, equality, and respect for all. But the more I learned, the more I realized that this sanitized version of Canadian history was a privilege, one that ignored the voices of those who had suffered most under colonial policies.

The discomfort I felt wasn't just about acknowledging the wrongs of the past; it was about realizing how deeply ingrained these issues still are. Education systems, for example, continue to perpetuate narratives that erase or distort Indigenous perspectives. This wasn't just a problem of the past but a reflection of the ongoing challenges in how we talk about reconciliation, truth, and justice. How can we truly reconcile when the systems that shape our understanding of the world—our schools, our media, our public discourse—still operate from a place of ignorance or denial?

I've come to see that my immigrant experience, my desire to fit in and feel a part of this country, is a small part of a much bigger conversation. I wanted to be "Canadian", but I didn't fully understand what that meant. Now, I see that being Canadian isn't just about belonging to a multicultural mosaic; it's about recognizing the responsibilities we all share in addressing the injustices that continue to affect Indigenous communities. It's about asking ourselves what kind of future we want to build: A future that is truly inclusive, one that honors the truth rather than glossing over it.

For me, this journey of learning has been about more than guilt or shame. It's been about responsibility. It's not enough to simply know the truth; we have to ask ourselves what we're going to do with it.

How do we challenge the systems that have caused harm? How do we ensure that education becomes a tool for real understanding and change, rather than a means of maintaining the status quo?

As someone who has benefited from the opportunities Canada provides, I feel a deeper sense of accountability to help create space for the stories that haven't been told—stories that are central to what this country truly is and could be. We owe it to ourselves, to our children, and to the generations of Indigenous peoples who have carried these burdens for far too long. This isn't just a matter of reconciliation; it's a matter of reimagining the very foundations of what it means to be a part of this place, to learn from its past and work toward a future that is genuinely just.

In many ways, the more I understand this history, the more my love for this country has deepened; not in spite of its flaws, but because the path forward requires all of us to engage with the truth. It's a love rooted in the hope that we can do better, that we can build a nation that not only acknowledges its past but actively works to heal from it. That, to me, is the essence of what it means to belong to this land.

–

On this first National Day
for Truth and Reconciliation,
I stand with all Canadians,
bearing the guilt of a history
marked by loss and silence,
the innocent lives of Indigenous children
whose spirits still call for justice.
We are bound by the obligation
to grieve, to remember,

and to carry the weight of remorse,
for the lives lost, the futures stolen,
and the deep scars left behind.
In this moment, we commit
to accountability and retribution,
to the work that remains;
to heal, to rebuild,
a society where all are seen,
and the echoes of the past
no longer go unheard.

—Sincerely, Boris

The Places That You've Come To Fear The Most

There is a delicate art in facing fear. In the quiet spaces of my mind, I have often grappled with those deep-seated anxieties; the ones that linger beyond the obvious, like my childhood fears of heights, spiders, or bees. But fear, I've come to understand, is not simply an instinctual response; it is an illusion that seeks to disrupt our natural course, distorting reality and filling it with false limitations.

As I reflect on my personal fears, like the fear of disappointing those I love, the fear of being alone, or even the inevitable reality of death, I realize that these emotions, though real, are often exaggerated by a part of me that clings to control. They take root in uncertainty, feeding on the unknown, and that's where they derive their power. Yet the key to overcoming these fears lies not in fighting them directly, but in acknowledging them and seeing them for what they are: Illusions designed to keep me from my personal growth.

Fear of failure, of not living up to expectations, can be paralyzing. It has, at times, made me doubt my ability to be a good father or to navigate the complexities of relationships. But what I've learned is that fear does not define me. It may attempt to impose narratives about inadequacy or isolation, but these stories are not truths; they are interpretations. I do not have to live by them.

The first step is recognizing when fear begins to speak. In those moments, instead of letting it drive my actions, I can choose to stand firm in my understanding of self. Fear may try to whisper that I am alone, or that I might not be enough for those I hold dear, but I now realize that these whispers are merely echoes of past insecurities. They are not the voice of my reality.

To truly cast out fear, I must strip away its falsehoods, stand grounded in my values, and recognize my strength, not in spite of fear, but because I have faced it. By dismantling the illusion, I can step forward confidently, knowing that while fear may exist, it holds no dominion over my choices, my identity, or my future.

In this understanding, I reclaim a more profound sense of peace. Fear is simply a shadow. And while it may darken parts of my journey, it can never overcome the light of my inner strength unless I let it. The power lies within me to confront fear, not with force, but with clarity. And in that clarity, fear begins to dissolve.

—

In the darkness where fear resides,
A whisper calls, a truth confides.
Don't flee the shadows, don't turn away;
Embrace the fear, let it have its say.

In uncertainty's grip, we often freeze,
Yet within that tightness lies the key to ease.
Open your heart, let the emotion of fear flow.
In vulnerability, true courage will grow.

Fear, a teacher with lessons so profound.
In the quiet depths, strength can be found.
Befriend the fear, dance with its might;
For when the moment passes,
we will see the light.

I was born into a world of fear,
Where I grew up to hide my tears.
No steady hands to guide my way,
Only scattered paths I learned to face.
In madness, I sought to comprehend
A life that shifted without end.

I grew too fast, too much to bear,
The weight of truths placed in my care.
Yet through the bruises, I made my stand,
A way to live beyond demand.

No longer tied to what was given,
I carved a path, my own, forgiven.
It wasn't just to survive the fall,
But to rise and live beyond it all.

Kindness starts within,
where wounds are tender.
When you heal yourself,
you'll understand others better.

Stay present in the moments
when pain calls your name.
Don't flee, don't fight; just stay.
In stillness, strength is quietly gained.

Let your heart remain open,
no matter how it feels.
In the practice of courage,
your spirit gently heals.

—Sincerely, Boris

Ballad Of Firsts

The day was bright, the air was sweet.
Beneath the trees, their eyes did meet.
With blush and smile, they stepped in line,
Then fingers twined and hands entwined.
Her hand in his, his heart a-race,
A warmth bloomed in that secret space.
They walked and laughed and felt so light,
As closeness grew with pure delight.
A moonlit night, soft voices stilled,
And with one glance, their breaths were filled.
A daring tilt, their faces near,
First kiss alight; both bold, sincere.
Then candles low and shadows cast,
Two souls as one, no future, past.
They held, they kissed, they drifted deep,
In love's first dance; a playful leap.
So hand-in-hand, with stars above,
They found the spark and called it love.
In steps so new, yet sure and right,
They made a world in one soft night.

—Sincerely, Boris

My Resting Place

I dream of a home by a quiet lake,
Where trees surround, and the air I take
Is filled with the scent of fresh-brewed grace;
Black coffee rises as I wake.
Inside, the rooms glow with memories,
Stories of love, of hope, of peace;
Each wall bears stains of joy, long pressed,
And pillows, blankets, throws made of cotton and fleece.

The kitchen, warm; a hearth for all,
Where stomachs are full and laughter calls;
Conversations linger, soft and sweet,
As friends and family share their seats.
The walls are littered with art that brings
A reflection of life, of the little things;
Moments captured, frozen in bliss
Like the image of our very first kiss.

A library waits, its wisdom always near,
Photo albums filled with memories so clear;
A treasury of knowledge close at hand,
Stories shared with the closest of friends.
The pantry brims with all we need
To craft each meal, to plant each seed;
Enough to nourish an endless fire,
A feast for love's unquenched desire.

Outside, a garden stretches wide,
Green with life, where dreams reside;
Tall trees shade a tranquil view
Of water glistening, bright and true.
A wooden dock cradles our boat.
Together we drift, we dream, we float;
From one soft moment to the next one,
Our love is the current,
Reminding us where we've come from.

Beneath the sun, a spot I find,
To write, to read, to free my mind;
The space to dream, to plant, to grow,
To craft the life I've come to know.
The grass a canvas, green and bright,
A valley of hope, a dream in flight
Where changing thoughts take solid form,
New ideas and themes are born.

And as the stars like fireflies glow,
We sit by the fire's final show;
The flames die down, the embers fade,
And call us to our peaceful shade.
I dream of a home by a quiet lake
Where we are proud of the life we make.

—Sincerely, Boris

Mending A Broken Heart

This past year has been one of the hardest, as I've had to navigate the pain of getting over someone I deeply loved. The journey of mending a broken heart has been anything but straightforward. Yet through the struggle, I've found that healing isn't about erasing the love I felt, but about rediscovering myself through the loss.

Heartbreak forces me to confront vulnerability and unearth the resilience that often goes unnoticed in times of happiness. I've learned that love, in its intensity, is not just about giving, but also knowing when to let go.
True healing begins not when I forget the person, but when I grow beyond the shadow of the relationship. It's a process of cultivating self-compassion and nurturing independence, not by denying the pain, but by embracing it. Through suffering, I forge new strength.

Moving forward requires a shift in perspective. Rather than seeing the end of love as failure, I now view it as a transition into self-discovery. It's an opportunity to reevaluate my values, redefine my aspirations, and focus on the life I wish to create: One rooted in joy, purpose, and fulfillment. Growth may be uncomfortable, but it is through discomfort that I flourish.

I've come to understand that love does not abandon; it transforms. It invites me to love myself more fully, to seek happiness from within, and to anchor my well-being in my own spirit. Closure isn't a single moment; it's a series of small releases, each loosening the grip of the past.

The first step is acceptance; acknowledging that love, like all things, changes. What once connected us now drifts us apart, not out of malice, but from the natural course of life. We are beings in motion, evolving, and sometimes our paths diverge.

I've learned to embrace the silence that follows absence. It's tempting to fill the void with distractions, but in solitude, I've found clarity. Sitting with my pain and letting it unravel at its own pace has shown me that the heart has an incredible capacity for healing when given the space to breathe. Each tear is a testament to the depth of my love, not a weakness.

Time, I've realized, isn't the healer; awareness is. Time will pass regardless, but it's the moments of self-reflection and introspection that allow me to break free from old memories. Pain is not a punishment but a lesson, each heartbreak teaching me more about myself, my desires, and the love I want and deserve.

Moving on is, in its own way, an act of faith. It requires me to let go of the past and open my heart to the unknown, trusting that something new awaits. In the gentle release, I've found peace. By not clinging to what was, I've made space for what might be.

The greatest lesson, though, is that love doesn't belong to anyone but myself. The love I gave and received remains within me, undiminished. Though the person I shared it with is no longer beside me, the essence of that love is a part of who I am and who I will continue to become.

This journey has taught me that getting over someone isn't about forgetting them; it's about remembering who I am without them. It's about finding the strength to move forward, with grace, knowing that love will find me again, perhaps when I least expect it.

—

Healing isn't forgetting,
It's growing through the loss.
Love changes, not abandons,
And I rediscover myself.
In silence, clarity sprouts;
Each tear is a mark of strength.
Moving on means letting go,
And making space for what's next.

—Sincerely, Boris

Heartfelt Sincerity

In every heartbeat, I choose you.
With every breath, I let you go.

—Sincerely, Boris

Limerence

The experience of growing up always in the grip of fleeting desires has shaped how I approach relationships, even now, as a single father in my forties. I've often found myself captivated by the allure of infatuation, swept away by the idealized image of another person. This pattern, though intoxicating, has taught me much about the nature of desire and the way it distorts reality.

I've come to see that these intense feelings—what I once thought was love—are often projections of my own unmet needs or desires onto another person. These crushes, which often felt overwhelming, were more about the fantasy I created than the reality of the person in front of me. I've learned that this yearning is less about genuine connection and more about the emotional highs I sought to escape from my own inner discomforts or unfulfilled longings.

With time, I've begun to understand the importance of self-awareness in these moments. What feels like love can sometimes be a fixation on an idealized version of someone, built from the fragments of my own hopes and unresolved emotions. True connection, I've realized, must be grounded in seeing the other person as they are, not as a reflection of what I want them to be.

In this journey, I've learned to let go of the compulsive need to chase after those fleeting feelings and instead nurture a deeper, more balanced emotional availability. It is about cultivating a sense of wholeness within myself, so that I no longer need another person to fill a void or complete me. This shift has been liberating, though it requires constant reflection and conscious effort. The path forward is not about denying desire but understanding its true source and embracing relationships that allow for growth, mutual respect, and authenticity.

—

Your name constant, lingering in my mind;
All the thoughts of you, I cannot escape.
They echo through time,
where a lonely silence once found its place.

In your eyes, I can I see beyond the universe,
its vastness reflected in their cosmic depths,
where time slows down, remains suspended,
revealing truths I hadn't thought to seek.

And in your touch, oh, how it lingers;
a quiet fire that burns without need for flame.
It consumes all of me, drawing me closer to you,
where distance stretches, one galaxy to another,
Until I am lost in the warmth of your being.

You are the axis on which my thoughts turn,
the light that bends the edges of my soul.
Yet I know this;
to love you is not to possess,
but to admire the art in simply knowing
you exist, a masterpiece worth holding onto.

You are the one question I cannot answer,
a riddle unraveling in my mind everyday.

—Sincerely, Boris

My Twin Brother

You were the first face I knew,
A silent companion in our mother's womb;
Nine months shared in a quiet, unseen world.
On a warm August day in eighty-three, we emerged,

Minutes apart, yet bound by something remarkable.
In our childhood, we clung to one another,
Guarding each other from the darkness,
Our scars woven from shared mischief,
Every scrape, every sickness, every consequence
ours alone.

We were partners in play:
Morning cartoons, pro wrestling, collecting trading cards,
and console wars with thrills of every extra life we won
together.
We threw the ball, rode our bikes,
And set fire to the world in reckless joy.

Our bedroom, a small universe,
furnished with our bunk bed stacked high,
walls covered in our silly dreams,
matching outfits in spirit, in rivalry, in victories and defeats.

Through the storms and the quiet, we never truly parted;
No matter how far the distance between us,
We have always found our way back to one another.

There were moments of silence,
of misunderstandings, of words lost in the air,
Yet we weathered through hunger and fought our battles as
a team, and though at times we faltered, we were never lost.

We shared more than a birthday,
More than a sister, a father, a mother.
We shared dreams, our first car,
and fleeting glimpses of doubts and fear.

To this day, you remain my hero,
The closest friend, the unbreakable tie;
No matter where life leads us,
We are, always, one.

And as I look back on the journey we've traveled,
I am filled with pride, for how far we've come;
Together still. No matter what.

—Sincerely, Boris

Questionnaire

What were you doing,
in those years of stillness,
while I carried the weight alone?

How could you sleep
in the warmth of our bed,
knowing I spent eight years
cold on the floor of the den?

What value did you bring
to this hollow marriage,
while I gave, and you took,
until there was nothing left?

Fourteen years;
you took it all,
and now, in the silence of "after",
you want even more.

Why no passion?
No spark beyond the glow of the TV?
Was there never anything inside you
But emptiness?

You tried to twist my reflection,
cast me as the villain,
the bad father, the bad husband,
but your words were untruthful.

Why didn't you work?
Was your paper degree
just another thing left to dust?

Why that awful tone,
and why so much care
for the judgment of strangers,
when I stood beside you, unseen?

What do you even tell them,
those who ask why I left?

And what of our daughter?
What will she think
of this shattered past,
these unanswered questions?

Can you just leave me
with this silence, the peace,
and move on?

—Sincerely, Boris

Cycles Of My Past

I learned that true healing begins with the recognition of the patterns passed down through generations, woven into the fabric of my emotional life. My childhood experiences, whether painful or nurturing, have shaped my responses to the world, and only by acknowledging the wounds left behind can I begin to free myself from their grip. I must confront the destructive behaviours that have taken root, those subtle habits of self-sabotaging and deeply-ingrained fears that seem to guide my actions almost unconsciously.

To move forward, I take responsibility for my emotional growth. This journey requires me to nurture the parts of myself that have been neglected, to offer the care and compassion that were once missing. I have learned to cultivate an inner sense of safety, to build trust within myself, and to challenge the narratives that no longer serve me. Through deliberate self-exploration, I identify the beliefs and emotions that have kept me stuck, and I work to transform them into my greatest strengths.

It's a process of reparenting; providing myself with the love, guidance, and protection I once sought from others. I gently untangle myself from the trauma that has echoed across generations, and in doing so, I begin to break free from the cycles of the past. Each step forward brings me closer to a more resilient, authentic version of myself, one that is capable of self-empowerment and emotional growth. This isn't a journey of quick fixes but one of deep transformation, where I learn to honour my past while fully embracing the potential of who I am becoming.

—

I listen closely to his cry,
A truth long hidden, now untied.
With love, I heal the aching past,
And offer peace that's meant to last.

I break the hold of old belief,
Release the pain, embrace relief.
In every tear, in every plea,
I find the strength to set him free.

I draw my boundaries firm and clear,
Protect the space that I hold dear.
With quiet strength, no longer torn,
The child within me has been reborn.

—Sincerely, Boris

The Essence Of Leadership

Navigating the dynamics of leadership has taught me a delicate balance: How to hold authority in one hand and approachability in the other. Each day in my role as a marketer and strategist invites me to refine that balance further, understanding that leadership isn't merely a title but a commitment to my personal and professional growth, and that of those whom I lead and mentor.

In my experience, the essence of leading isn't found in directives alone. It's about fostering trust, encouraging voices to speak, and welcoming perspectives that challenge my own. I've learned to listen deeply, particularly when emotions flare or tensions rise. Handling conflict, I realize, is a test of patience and empathy: A time to pause, recalibrate, and focus on a resolution that prioritizes both humanity and purpose.

Confidence in leadership, I've come to find, isn't about being the loudest in the room but the most attuned. It's about delivering a vision with clarity, rooted in the same storytelling techniques that have shaped my career as a strategist. The art of uncovering and conveying insights in media mirrors the art of leading; both require an authentic connection to audiences that resonates deeply.

And just as I've mentored others, the journey has revealed how vital my own mentors have been. They've shown me how to integrate integrity into every decision, balance decisiveness with sensitivity, and, perhaps most importantly, lead with resilience and humility. Through each experience, I've been reminded that to lead well is to serve a purpose greater than oneself, to cultivate a team that thrives as much on shared ambition as on shared respect.

—

I rose from roots that held me low,
With questions that the wise bestow;
A spark, a seed, a slow ascent,
To lead, to learn, and to relent.

In quiet halls where silence lay,
I gathered courage day by day,
And through each step, I came to find
The weight of heart, the power of mind.

Now, with open hands, I pass,
The flame to those who dare to ask;
For those who lead with humble grace
Will leave a path no time can erase.

—Sincerely, Boris

Teachable Moments

In my journey through mentorship and leadership, I have discovered that teaching is a profound exchange where clarity and engagement become essential. Unlike many of my peers, I wasn't afforded the privilege of higher education. Yet this gap ignited a deep curiosity within me, compelling me to seek knowledge through every available resource, both within and beyond the workplace. Each book, conference, white-paper, training module, conversation, and experience became a stepping stone, offering insights that transformed learning into teachable moments.

As I navigated the world of media and advertising, my passion for storytelling emerged as a guiding force. My experiences reveal a commitment to crafting narratives that resonate with audiences, whether through creative campaigns or impactful presentations. I believe that every interaction is an opportunity to illuminate complex ideas and inspire others to engage with them meaningfully.

Throughout my career, I have embraced the role of mentor, nurturing the growth of those around me. I've witnessed how the joy of discovery can spark motivation in individuals, understanding that teaching is not merely about imparting knowledge but about cultivating an environment that encourages questions and fosters exploration. Each presentation and public speaking engagement has allowed me to connect with others and unravel complexities with elegance, illuminating paths to understanding.

Reflecting on the exceptional mentors who have shaped my path, I recognize the wisdom that has been passed down to me. Their guidance has equipped me to navigate challenges with purpose and clarity, reinforcing my commitment to creating inclusive spaces where minds can thrive.

These experiences have not only shaped my professional life but also prepared me to teach my daughter. My journey has instilled in me the confidence to share knowledge and nurture her curiosity. As I guide her through the complexities of life, I draw upon my own learning journey, using my insights from both my personal and professional life to emphasize the importance of resilience and creativity. In every interaction, I strive to inspire a love for learning, fostering an environment where she can explore, question, and grow, just as I have throughout my own path.

—

In the skies, a graceful flight,
A formation of geese takes to the light.
With honks that echo, a call to align,
Each bird is a beacon, their purpose divine.

If one stumbles, strays from the way,
The others adjust, a united ballet.
Together they rise, through storm and through sun,
Learning from missteps, for they are as one.

In the dance of their wings, a lesson unfolds
In the warmth of their hearts, a wisdom that holds.
For in every falter, a chance to inspire,
A chance to grow stronger, to reach even higher.

As leaders, we guide, but in falling, we learn
To embrace our mistakes, and for growth, we yearn.
Like the geese in the sky, let our voices unite—
In formation, we thrive, together in flight.

—Sincerely, Boris

Seven Minutes In Heaven

It was the seventh grade, and I had begun exchanging notes with a girl I found myself thinking about between every class. There was a certain innocence in those notes, little windows into our youthful curiosity about one another. At a friend's birthday party, we played a game that felt monumental at the time: Seven Minutes in Heaven. We sat on opposite ends of the couch, the space between us buzzing with nervous anticipation, until our names were called. My heart raced as we stepped into the darkened closet, the world outside falling away.

In the quiet of that small space, I reached for her hands, unsure and trembling. She leaned in gently, and as if drawn by a shared instinct, I followed. Our hands slowly parted, giving way to an embrace. What began as a shy, tentative kiss soon blossomed into something more; seven minutes of exploration, where the unfamiliar became familiar, and a first kiss unfolded into a world entirely new to me.

In that brief span of time, I discovered the sweet weight of connection, as though we'd uncovered some secret, unspoken yet understood. It was a moment both thrilling and terrifying, a tender initiation into the mysteries of affection.

—

I reached for you with hands
that had never known such trembling,
and you leaned in, soft as breath.

Together we crossed the thin line
between innocence and the edge of knowing.
In that quiet, our lips found each other,
tentative explorers of an undiscovered world.

Seven minutes stretched into forever,
as our hands fell away and we held on tighter;
a first kiss becoming seven minutes
of sweetness, of shared discovery.

—Sincerely, Boris

A Strength I Didn't Know Was Mine

In the pursuit of lasting, secure relationships, I find myself reflecting on how anxiety has left its subtle, often unspoken imprints across my life. Growing up with a distant relationship with my parents, I internalized early on a sense of unfulfilled attachment, the absence of closeness planting seeds of doubt and a yearning for validation. In the silence of those unmet needs, I began searching for the assurances I never received, hoping that connection could anchor me to something steady.

This desire for security led me into a marriage that, for fourteen years, became a mirror of my deepest fears rather than a refuge. Each day felt like an exercise in survival, measuring my worth against another's indifference, trying to reconcile my self-worth and patience with a relationship that drained rather than sustained. My anxieties flourished in that space; I was reaching for connection but grasping at emptiness. The experience taught me how profoundly loneliness can exist within a partnership and how silence can erode one's sense of self over time.

Today, as a single father to my daughter, I am determined to write a different story, to create a life for her filled with the presence and closeness I once craved. I want to show her that love can be secure and kind, that her worth is intrinsic and unshakeable. I am learning, slowly, to offer myself the same assurance I give to her, a steady reminder that my value is not dependent on another's approval or affection.

In this journey, I am coming to see that true security begins with me, with the quiet work of nurturing my resilience. Rather than allowing my fears to dictate my relationships, I am choosing to embrace them as part of my story, without letting them define its future. Each relationship now becomes an invitation to bring forward a more authentic, calm self. Through this process, I am becoming not only a more present father but a person capable of opening up without seeking guarantees. And in that vulnerability, I find a strength I never knew was mine.

—

In quiet moments, I can feel her near,
A light within the dark that holds me up,
Her laughter rising like the dawn's first breath,
A fragile warmth that steadies broken ground.
Through storms endured, I draw upon her spark,
Her gentle hand pressed firm against my own.
The innocence she guards with steady grace
Ignites a will to face the world once more.

I walk a road unkind and fierce at times,
Yet find my steps grow firm, my heart unbound,
For in her eyes I see a thousand suns;
Their heat is enough to melt the hardest of fears.

If ever strength were borne from flesh and bone,
Then mine arose when she took in her breath;
My will to fight, to stand when all seems lost,
Lies nestled safe within her boundless trust.

—Sincerely, Boris

Yummy pumpkin pies,
Red, orange, and yellow leaves,
I love the fall breeze.

—Sincerely, Macy

For In Surviving, I Am Victorious

In my pursuit of resilience and inner calm, I've come to realize that true freedom comes from focusing only on what I can control. Stoicism teaches me to accept hardships as opportunities for growth, transforming challenges into exercises for strengthening my character. By practicing moderation and temperance, I aim to live a life guided by reason, free from the sway of fleeting emotions.

Time is precious, and I strive to live with purpose, fully present and grateful for each moment. Embracing the impermanence of life, I seek to cultivate inner peace, knowing that my strength lies in how I respond to the world, not in the events themselves.

There are moments in life when the weight of existence feels unbearable, when darkness overwhelms every sense and the world appears void of meaning. In such times, it is easy to forget that pain is temporary, that despair can coexist with hope, even when hope is invisible. The journey through suffering is not linear, nor does it have a definitive end, yet through it, I learn that survival itself is a profound act of courage.

The mind, when entangled in anxiety and depression, becomes its own worst enemy, convincing me that the worst-case scenario is inevitable. Yet, in the midst of this battle, I am reminded that thoughts, as real as they feel, are not facts. I have learned to recognize the difference between reality and the false stories my mind tells me.

As I continue through these challenges, I realize that time, though intangible, is one of the greatest healers. What seems unbearable today will one day become a memory, softened by the passing of time. The strength to continue, to endure even when it feels impossible, lies in understanding that change is constant, and nothing, not even pain, is permanent.

Connection to others becomes a lifeline; shared stories, moments of vulnerability, and human kindness all serve as reminders that I am not alone. Through the darkness, there is beauty in simplicity: The warmth of a kind word, the stillness of a sunset, or the calm after a storm. These seemingly small things are powerful anchors that keep me grounded in the present, reminding me that life is worth holding onto.

I learn that happiness is not a goal to be reached but rather a series of fleeting moments that come and go. It's not about constant euphoria but about finding peace with the highs and lows. Ultimately, the greatest lesson is this: I must not be afraid of the struggle. For in surviving, in continuing, I am already victorious. Life, in all its complexity and pain, is worth living.

—

In the darkest hours, I learn
That pain will fade and not return.
Thoughts deceive, but time can heal,
And simple joys make life feel real.

Happiness is not a place,
But fleeting moments I will trace.
Through every breath, through every trial,
Surviving shows I've lived worthwhile.

In my quest for strength, I embrace stoicism,
Finding my way through life's challenges.
In chaos, I learn to remain steady;
True control lies beyond what I cannot change.

Each struggle shapes my will to grow,
In hardship, I uncover my resilience.
Grateful for both joy and pain,
I accept life as it comes.

With virtue and courage as my guides,
I walk a stoic path, steadfast and true.

—Sincerely, Boris

Effort Is Everything

I've come to realize that my efforts to thrive, whether in my career, health, or as a father, are deeply interconnected. Life's demands can sometimes feel overwhelming, but I've discovered that nurturing one area of my life ripples through others, creating a powerful synergy. When I prioritize sleep, for instance, I awaken with a clear mind and more energy, allowing me to be fully present in my work and with my daughter. A rested body and mind make decisions sharper, productivity smoother, and stress more manageable.

In the same way, nourishing my body through healthy eating fuels not only my physical vitality but also my mental resilience. I've found that what I put into my body directly influences how I approach challenges, both personal and professional. With a clear head, I'm able to remain patient and present, whether strategizing for a new project or supporting my daughter through a difficult moment.

Movement, too, is essential. I've experienced firsthand how physical activity not only strengthens the body but also clears emotional weight. Regular exercise not only boosts my energy but also reminds me of my inner strength; the same strength that has allowed me to overcome past hardships. It's a reminder that no matter how tough life can get, pushing through physical limits mirrors the mental and emotional perseverance needed to succeed.

Finally, the way I think—the conscious effort to cultivate positive, clear, and focused thoughts—shapes everything. My mind is like a garden, and I've learned to tend to it with the same care I apply to my relationships and career. A strong, intentional mindset is a cornerstone for success. When my mind is calm, I can face challenges in business with a strategic outlook, be a more thoughtful father, and handle the ups and downs of life with resilience.

As I reflect, it's clear that my ambitions—whether in my work, health, or as a parent—are not isolated efforts. Every decision, every habit, every mindful choice creates ripples that push me toward becoming the person I strive to be. Just as I work hard in my career to create a lasting impact, I'm also creating lasting effects within myself, ensuring that I continue to grow and thrive in every aspect of life.

—

Nothing speaks louder than effort,
A silent force that measures desire,
A spark that drives us to make things happen;
Whether selfish or selfless, it builds
Toward something greater than ourselves.

It is the universal tongue,
Spoken in every corner of the world,
Telling each other how much we care,
How deeply we long,
How badly we crave the outcome.

It anchors our actions with purpose,
Reaffirms our intentions with resolve.
When effort flows effortlessly,
When the will moves like instinct,
It tells the story of our aspirations,
Of the dreams we strive to bring to life.

Effort wears many faces,
But it always begins with you;
With what you seek to prove,
To yourself or someone of special,
Or even to the world at large.

—Sincerely, Boris

Servicing Connections

At the heart of the human experience lies the power of connection and the ways in which we service those around us. Through intentional acts of generosity, we create transformative moments that transcend the ordinary. The core of this philosophy teaches us that going beyond mere functionality in service or business is not just an option; it is a moral imperative. We should aim to offer not only what is expected but something far more greater: The gift of presence, empathy, and understanding.

Every interaction is an opportunity to make someone feel seen, valued, and celebrated. Whether in professional endeavors or personal relationships, the emphasis is placed on creating experiences that delight and surprise. This requires being fully present, understanding the deeper needs of others, and anticipating desires they might not have articulated themselves. To truly service someone is about crafting moments of unexpected joy, moments that people will carry with them long after the experience has passed.

The way we treat others is a way of living, a form of leadership, and an approach to community-building that nurtures both the giver and the receiver. By embracing humility, curiosity, and care, one can elevate the mundane to the extraordinary, creating environments where trust and loyalty naturally flourish.

It is never enough to merely satisfy; one must delight, inspire, and create something that reflects the highest form of respect for another's humanity. When we make the effort to connect on this deeper level, we not only foster meaningful relationships but also open doors to greater creativity, innovation, and fulfillment.

By infusing our work and lives with intentional acts of kindness and thoughtfulness, we can transform the world around us. In doing so, we honor the people we serve, and in turn, elevate our own lives to a state of purpose and joy.

—

The way we connect reflects our way of life:
A path of leadership, a bond of community,
Where both the giver and receiver thrive.

Embrace humility, curiosity, and care;
Elevate the mundane to the extraordinary,
Cultivating trust, nurturing loyalty's roots.

To satisfy is not our destined goal;
To delight and inspire, to honor the soul,
Creating a space that mirrors respect

Where humanity's essence is fully reflected.
In deep connection, we weave meaningful ties,
Opening doors to creativity, where innovation thrives.

With intention, we infuse our work and our days.
Acts of kindness transform in wondrous ways,
Honoring those we serve in heartfelt embrace,

Elevating our lives to a purpose-filled place.
In the fabric of giving, our joy is defined,
For in nurturing others, our own hearts unwind.

— Sincerely, Boris

Imperfections

There comes a point in life where we can no longer deny our own destruction, where we're forced to confront the ways in which we've dulled the pain, buried the truth, and lost control of ourselves. The allure of escaping reality, of numbing the heartache, can be intoxicating, but it comes at a cost: The slow decay of everything that once held meaning, including friendships, love, and purpose. There's a false sense of strength in pretending nothing is wrong, yet the more one tries to hold it all together, the further life unravels.

The path to sobriety, though agonizing, offers a painful but necessary mirror. It demands reckoning with not just the actions but the reasons behind them—the wounds we ignore, the fears we refuse to name, and the responsibilities we flee. In learning to accept the truth, we discover the importance of being accountable, not just to others, but to ourselves. Only through this raw confrontation do we begin to rebuild, piece by piece, a life that no longer needs to be hidden or numbed.

Ultimately, healing requires not just quitting the substances, but understanding why we turn to them in the first place. It's about discovering that despite our flaws, despite the failures and damage left in our wake, we are worthy of redemption and love. In the end, the greatest lesson is realizing that our imperfections do not define us; they can fuel our growth if we are brave enough to face them.

—

There comes a time to face the pain,
to see the cracks we've tried to hide,
numbing what once mattered most:
friendships, love, our sense of pride.

Healing isn't just letting go,
it's knowing why we turned to run.
Despite the scars, despite the fall,
we're still worthy of love.

—Sincerely, Boris

Crush

You found me when I needed to stir,
a spark to wake what had dimmed within.
In you, I see the change;
a light that makes me more myself
than I've felt in so long.
The thrill of your morning words,
your soft goodnight whispers,
bring me back to life,
reborn with hope,
alive in ways I'd forgotten.

Your stories, your curious heart,
your beauty, inside and out;
they beckon me to write,
to craft your essence in words
and share them with the world.
It's your kindness, your actions,
the effort you pour,
even the way your hair falls;
it stirs in me a feeling I thought
I had long since lost.

Your smile, your photographs,
the elegance with which you move;
I want to sit deep inside your mind
and map out every secret,
every last tender detail.
And now, I find myself wondering
what could bloom between us
if we keep walking this path,
keep sharing these moments?

The excitement pulls me forward
to see where our words,
our laughter, our hearts
might lead.
But even if our paths diverge,
if we drift or don't quite fit,
it was worth every moment;
to feel, to grow, to know you.
And no matter where we end,
I'll be there, cheering from the sidelines,
rooting for your light
to shine even brighter.

And it's your gentleness, your grace,
the way you wonder and care
that makes me rise before the sun,
to shape myself anew,
so you might have the best of me—
a part of me no one else can share.

—Sincerely, Boris

Bouquet Of Roses

She drives two hours through winding roads,
and every second, we're on the phone.
With fair skin kissed by the sun's embrace,
with blue eyes where skies are traced.

Her light brown hair falls soft and free,
with rosy cheeks; a bouquet just for me.
Her smile lifts, her cheekbones high,
a beauty so rare, like stars in the night sky.

She stands strong, a mother with passion,
her little boy's world, and a sense of fashion.
With hands that tend a garden wide,
and a chicken coop by her countryside.

She knows the names of trees and stars,
and holds close the world with open arms.
A heart so kind, and wise, and true,
her laughter brightens all it moves through.

Through late-night calls, sharing favorite bands,
minutes turn hours under her graceful hands.
Her messages rings throughout the day,
and I keep her photos, in my phone they lay.

So here's to her beauty, her strength, her grace,
to our shared hours, spent face-to-face.
No matter the miles or years that divide,
I'll hold her image close, by my side.

—Sincerely, Boris

Love Life

Throughout my life, I have experienced three distinct kinds of romantic love.

The First Love–

My first love came in high school, a fluttery feeling filled with exploration and friendship. It was here that I learned to say "I love you" for the first time. This love introduced me to the pain of heartbreak, leaving me with a sense of emptiness that felt insurmountable. Yet it set me on a path toward future relationships, teaching me that love can also be a beginning.

The Second Love–

The second kind of love demands deep investment of time, effort, and emotion. It paints a picture of a promising partnership but often ends in disappointment. After fourteen years in a marriage, I came to realize that I was not truly in love; I was captivated by the idea of love itself. This experience taught me important lessons about how I want to give and receive love, but it also left me with a sense of regret, highlighting the difference between genuine connection and mere potential.

The Third Love-

The third type of love arrives naturally, without force. This rare love invites us to give our whole selves to someone deserving. While it can lead to deep emotional consequences when lost, when cherished, it has the power to flourish into something profound. This love encourages growth, inspiring us to become better versions of ourselves, both for our partners and for our own sake. This is the type of love you hold onto as tightly as possible. Losing the third love can be the most painful, leaving an indelible mark as a reminder of what true love means. This is the love we beg to take us back. Until it's gone forever.

Many of us are fortunate to experience one or two of these loves, and each journey prepares us for the next. I hope to one day find a fourth kind of love one day, but for now, I embrace the lessons learned from all three. Each has shaped my understanding of true love, true loss, regret, happiness, and the way I wish to connect with others.

—Sincerely, Boris

—

Act One:

It takes a year to learn loss,
to feel the weight of each day without its rhythm,
what once was is now only a shadow;
what was here has slipped away.

It takes a year to understand the space
you still hold in my heart, in my mind.
What was once hollow now aches with memory.
What was once vacant is now filled with longing.

It takes a year to fall in love,
and a moment to take it for granted.
What was once ours has drifted beyond reach.
What was once ours belongs to the past.

It takes a year to regret the deepest mistake,
to lose everything; even yourself.
What was once within grasp is now gone,
what once was life is now distant.

It takes a year to mourn the loss,
to feel again what was missed and forgotten.
What once broke me has now faded,
what once shattered is now still.

It takes a year to feel the sting of absence,
to realize the love you held is no longer yours,
and in the stillness of that truth, we find peace,
carving space for new beginnings for what's to come.

Act Two:

One year ago today,
I spoke those words that
I never thought I'd say again—
'I love you'—and in that moment,
My world had forever changed.

—Sincerely, Boris

Path To Self-Mastery

Many of my struggles stem not from external forces but from within, from patterns of self-sabotage that I once thought were beyond my control. It's recently become very clear to me that these moments of inner resistance I have struggled with, these times when I seem to work against my own best interests, are not random. They are my mind and body's way of protecting me from what feels unfamiliar or too overwhelming to face.

Personal growth, I've come to realize, has demanded not only patience but also the courage to confront these barriers inside of me. The obstacles I encounter aren't meant to be avoided or fought. Rather, they are reminders that within every challenge, there's an invitation to dig deeper, to look at my doubts, anxieties, and limiting beliefs, and to dismantle them.

This journey of mine is about mastering myself, not in the sense of becoming perfect, but in learning to be compassionate with my flaws, understanding where they come from, and allowing the proper space for my own evolution. I've learned that healing and progress come when I stop seeing my emotions as problems to fix and begin seeing them as messages guiding me toward what I truly need.

The transformation comes in the shift from self-sabotage to self-mastery. It requires me to take responsibility, to recognize that I am both the source of my struggles and the architect of my liberation. With this awareness, I can start to rebuild, step by step, by accepting where I am, forgiving myself for past mistakes, and slowly reorienting my life toward what truly aligns with my purpose. Mastery is not control; it is surrender to personal growth.

—

I am the mountain I must climb;
The stone I stumble on is mine.
Not to resist, but to take place
The path ahead, I must face.

The fear I feel, the doubt I bear,
Are voices calling for self-repair.
In every challenge, a chance to rise,
To meet the truth behind disguise.

The road is long, the path I'll clear,
With every step I dissolve the fear.
For in each wound, I heal and grow,
My heart learning what the mind can't know.

—Sincerely, Boris

Breaking The Cycle Of Mental Illness

I have come to understand that the burdens I carry—my anxiety, the emotional wounds that have shaped me—are not entirely mine to bear. They stretch back through generations, woven into the very fabric of my being, long before I was even born. The struggles of my ancestors, their unresolved trauma, echo in my life in ways that are both intimate and profound, manifesting in my thoughts, my body, and even my heart.

The breakdown of my marriage, the unbearable stress that contributed to the loss of my left eye, and the need for brain surgery were not simply the product of my own failings or missteps. There is a deeper inheritance at play, one that transcends my personal history. My ancestors' unresolved pain has rippled down through time, influencing how I navigate relationships, respond to stress, and even how my body has responded to the pressures around me.

The beauty of this understanding is that it does not absolve me of responsibility but offers clarity; a path to healing. I can look back with compassion, not only for myself but for the generations that came before me, who survived in ways they knew how, passing down their fears, their coping mechanisms, and their unspoken grief. In recognizing this legacy, I am called to break the cycle, to not pass this unresolved pain onto my daughter.

It is possible to heal, to release what is not truly mine, and in doing so, free myself and future generations. The memories of trauma that live in the body can be rewritten, the patterns of suffering interrupted. Healing does not mean erasing the past; it means transforming it, allowing me to finally breathe without the weight of centuries on my chest. It means standing in the present moment, aware of the lineage that shaped me but no longer bound by it.

This journey of healing requires more than awareness; it demands courage, presence, and the willingness to confront inherited pain. But through this process, I can cultivate resilience, transforming the energy of survival into one of creation and possibility. In learning to love myself, free from the ghosts of the past, I can offer my daughter the gift of a future unburdened by wounds that are not hers to carry. Through this work, I honor my ancestors by refusing to allow their suffering to define me or my legacy.

—

Beyond Labels—
We wear the names they give,
but beneath each title,
a story lives;
distinct, unspoken, unseen.
We are more than a diagnosis,
more than numbers or scales,
we are hearts stitched with hope,
souls searching for their own light.

The Winding Road—
Healing does not move in straight paths;
it curves and shifts,
sometimes pausing in silent moments.
It is shaped by hands that guide us,
by voices that hear,
by a world that often forgets
how to care beyond its walls.

Empathy's Reach—
Not just for those they label;
empathy is a mirror for all,
reflecting our fragile selves,
our hidden fears,
the cracks in our armor.
In each heart,
a quiet ache waits to be held.

Redefining Normal–
What is normal, but a mask,
a word that confines
What does it mean to be alive?
We build new definitions
through love, through struggle,
through the shared understanding
that none of us walk alone.

—Sincerely, Boris

Dharma

Human life often revolves around four pairs of opposites: Pleasure and pain, gain and loss, fame and disgrace, praise and blame. These desires and aversions become the forces that pull us through joy and sorrow, lifting us with hope only to sprint against fear.

We chase after pleasure and praise, fearful of the sting of pain or the shadow of disgrace. But this pursuit traps us in a cycle, never allowing us to rest in the present. Our hearts become tethered to outcomes, fluctuating with the forces of fortune.

True freedom lies not in the escape from these worldly concerns, but in the quiet awareness of their gravitational pull. By observing without attachment, we can step beyond the waves of desire and fear, finding stillness amidst the ever-shifting currents. Peace comes not in controlling the world but in loosening our grip, allowing joy and sorrow to pass like clouds in an endless sky.

Only then can we live with equanimity, untethered from the need to run away.

—Sincerely, Boris

Siddhartha

He sought the truth in whispered prayer,
In holy chants, in silence there,
But wisdom's voice eluded still,
A deeper call, a higher will.

He walked with saints, their words like gold,
Yet none could make his spirit whole.
No teacher's path, no master's way
Could light the truth he craved each day.

In pleasure's arms, he sought to see
The fleeting joys of ecstasy,
But wealth and wine could not fulfill
The endless thirst he carried still.

At the river's edge, he came to know
Life's rhythm in its constant flow.
The world, a dance of joy and pain,
Of loss, of birth, and all the same.

In every drop, in every breath,
He learned that life defies all death.
The river taught what none could say:
That wisdom blooms when we give way.

No truth can live in words alone;
It lives in hearts, in paths unknown.
To seek, to fall, to rise once more,
This was the lesson at the core.

—Sincerely, Boris

Quests Are Personal

I find that meaning comes not from the pursuit of happiness as a singular goal, but from the journey of seeking something greater than myself. I've come to understand that a quest, whether grand or humble, is what gives structure and intention to life. It's not merely about what I achieve but about the way in which I push my boundaries and challenge my comfort. The richness of life is woven through this constant pursuit, where the process itself brings fulfillment, growth, and ultimately, a deeper sense of purpose.

I've learned that quests are personal, and they vary from person to person. For some, it may be an exploration of the world; for others, an internal journey of self-mastery or spiritual enlightenment. What matters is not the specific nature of the journey but the fact that it demands something of me. A quest calls for sacrifice, resilience, and a willingness to embrace discomfort in the name of something meaningful. It teaches me to value perseverance and to cherish progress as much as the outcome.

In my experience as a divorced single father, I've found that even in failure or setback, there is an immense value in the effort. Each step forward, each obstacle, and each victory, no matter how small, brings clarity. I learn more about myself, about my limits, and about the world around me. This process has shown me that I am capable of more than I often imagine.

The most profound lesson I've come to understand is that life is more than the routine we fall into. It's about actively choosing a path that resonates with who I am at my core. The choice is to embark on a journey that allows me to live intentionally, to craft a story that is uniquely mine, and to pursue a legacy that matters—not necessarily to the world at large, but to my soul and for my daughter.

In seeking a quest, I've come to realize the importance of listening to the call of my heart and not the expectations of others. What is most true and beautiful in life is discovered through action, not merely contemplation. The quest is not about perfection; it is about daring greatly, facing fears, and allowing passion to guide me toward something meaningful. And through this pursuit, I find not just a fleeting sense of happiness, but a life that is rich in purpose.

—

I walk the path alone, not lost—
A father's heart, the cost embossed.
With one eye gone, I see more clear
The wounds of home, the quiet fear.

Through surgeries, through love undone,
The quest began when I was young.
Not in the joy, but in the pain,
I found my strength, I learned to reign.

A daughter's light, my guiding star,
Through a broken past, we've come so far.
This life, my journey, ever fast;
A quest for peace, for love that lasts.

—Sincerely, Boris

Becoming More: My Transformation Journey

This year has been a quiet transformation for me, a time where I've begun to understand that real change happens not through external shifts, but in the subtle reshaping of my inner world. I've come to see that the moments I once perceived as endings, like losing my left eye to glaucoma, going through brain aneurysm surgery, or leaving a toxic marriage, were, in truth, new beginnings waiting to unfold; disguised opportunities for growth.

One of the hardest lessons I've learned is that life's turning points aren't always dramatic. Instead, they arrive in moments of quiet clarity, where I learn to see fear as a doorway rather than an obstacle, and discomfort as a space where transformation is born. It was fear that kept me from leaving a toxic marriage. But I see now that it's also fear that drives us to transform. Discomfort, I've found, is where true growth happens. With this understanding, I've started to let go of narratives and habits that no longer serve me, embracing the idea that stepping into the unknown is less about losing and more about creating space for what I truly desire.

Letting go has become a necessary part of my journey. There is a certain elegance in the act of letting go; not as an abandonment, but as a necessary surrender. But in that surrender, I've discovered space to create something new. Becoming a father to my beautiful daughter has been the most beautiful creation of all, and she reminds me daily of the love that is still possible, despite the past. The necessary surrender is an opening, a way of allowing something new and authentic to take place. I now understand that if I want my life to reflect the desires of my heart, the work begins within me. Self-awareness, acceptance, and a commitment to nurturing my potential are what guide me forward.

As an immigrant, I've spent much of my life trying to prove myself, to belong. Time, I once thought, was a race—a linear path that demanded success, productivity, and validation. But after facing my own fragility in the operating room and enduring the loss of one of my closest friends, I've begun to see time as a fluid companion. Each day is an opportunity to realign with what truly matters. I'm no longer chasing external approval. I understand now that my worth lies in the depth of my connection to myself, to my daughter, and to the world around me.

I've found peace in embracing life's transitions. These transitions have shown me that there is strength in vulnerability, wisdom in uncertainty, and grace in allowing life to unfold as it will. I've learned that I can adapt, evolve, and meet life's inevitable changes with openness. Despite the hardships—growing up in an unhappy home, enduring surgeries, heartbreak, and loss—there is beauty in embracing life as it comes. There is power in knowing that, even in the face of all that has been, I am still capable of becoming more.

—

In heart's dark corners, a quiet voice is found;
love sprouts in the darkness, then falls to the ground.
A self once forgotten, shaped by love's art,
brought out by a muse, then torn apart.

The ache of becoming, the joy of decay,
a fragile heart lost and remade in a day.
In love's awakening aftermath, he stands alone,
wearing a version both fleeting and known.

—Sincerely, Boris

A Haiku: Glaucoma

It was all fun & games,
Until I lost my left eye.
Glaucoma prevailed.

—Sincerely, Boris

Forgiveness Clears My Path Forward

In moments when life feels burdensome, I've come to understand that my strength is not merely a defense against hardship but a promise I uphold: A daily act of courage in the face of adversity. There's a quiet power in holding my head up high. This simple act holds a deeply rooted bravery: The bravery to stand tall, to see my life with more clarity, and to meet my truth openly.

I've realized that my confidence is not found in grand gestures or external praise. Rather, it lives in the small, deliberate choices I have been making each day. It's in choosing to speak when silence feels easier, in standing firm when it would be simpler to retreat, and in reaching out despite the scars of my past. True strength, I've learned, is not the absence of fear but the determination to keep going in spite of it. And patience becomes my greatest ally here; patience with myself as I grow, with others as they walk their own paths, and with time, which gradually reveals meaning in its own way.

Forgiveness, too, is essential to this journey of mine. Yet forgiving others is only part of it; it's also about showing compassion to myself, letting go of bitterness and resentment that can silently weigh me down. In choosing to forgive, I free myself, creating room for growth and understanding. Forgiveness allows me to reclaim my energy and peace, unburdened by past pain.

Gratitude, then, becomes not just a practice but a new way of seeing. It's about recognizing the worth in what I have and in who I am becoming, even on the days when progress seems hidden or my direction uncertain. Every experience, whether joyful or challenging, has offered me insights that have deepened my strength. I learn to value not only the moments of achievement but also the marks left by past struggles, for they remind me of my journey, of battles overcome, and of my ability to rise, again and again.

The key for me has been to foster a genuine love for life, a love that endures through doubts and setbacks. It's a reminder that I am whole as I am, and that life's true beauty lies not in perfection but in the richness of each experience, in the quiet gift of being here. Through this understanding, I hold my head high; not from pride, but from a quiet, lasting faith in my path forward and in the person I am becoming.

—

When life bears down, I choose to stand;
A quiet resolve, a promise kept.
In simple acts, courage grows;
A word spoken, a hand reached,
Steps taken in patient trust.
Forgiveness clears what bitterness clouds,
And in gratitude, my view expands;
I find worth in scars, strength in soft places.
I walk this path, imperfect but whole,
My head held high, not from pride
But from faith in becoming.

—Sincerely, Boris

Deeper Understanding Of Love

I've come to understand that healing from a breakup is not merely about moving on, but about transforming loss into an opportunity for self-growth. The hardest lesson was the necessity of letting go completely; closing every door to the past, not to escape, but to confront the emptiness it had left behind. In mourning the end of the relationship, I also had to mourn the version of myself I had lost along the way; and accepting that the future we had planned would never come to pass. This loss was not just of what was, but of what could have been. Yet through time and the hard work of healing, I've found peace with this reality. Letting go of what was never meant to be has created space for new possibilities.

Setting new boundaries became essential. I learned that protecting my heart and mind required a lot of discipline, not as a defense, but as a way to reclaim my energy and direct it inward. In doing so, I realized that self-care isn't indulgence; it is the deliberate act of rebuilding my sense of worth.

One of the most important lessons I learned was accountability. I had to take responsibility for my choices, both in the relationship and in my healing. While forgiving myself for past mistakes was essential, even more crucial was holding myself to a higher standard moving forward. I began to clearly distinguish between love and attachment, between desire and need. Through this process, my perception of my ex shifted significantly, leaving me to question much about our past. It has been liberating to finally break free from the heartbreak that once consumed me.

As I worked to rebuild my self-esteem, I reawakened parts of me that had been silenced, rediscovering who I was before and who I could potentially become. Heartbreak, rather than something to avoid, became a refining force, shaping me into a stronger and more resilient version of myself.

As I rebuild my life and shape the future I now desire, I remain optimistic. I trust that love will find me again, and I will never give up on that journey. The pain has been my teacher, guiding me toward a deeper understanding of love, and preparing me for what lies ahead.

—

From our end, I found my start,
Fixing the pieces of my broken heart.
Heartbreak taught me to look within,
To face the pain beneath my skin.

In the torment, I learned to see
That love was never about you and me.
What once was broken is now whole;
In losing you, I've regained my soul.

No longer bound to what is gone,
I rise, renew, and carry on.
The heart that ached has learned to mend;
In its healing, I find my strength once again.

—Sincerely, Boris

Luctor et emergo

I've come to learn that patience is one of the greatest gifts I can give to my daughter's growth and learning. Her development rarely follows the path I expect, and there are times when it feels like progress is slow or even nonexistent. But I've seen firsthand that it is in those moments of struggle where the real growth happens.

There's a saying, *luctor et emergo*, "I struggle and emerge", and it's taught me that it is through facing difficulties that my daughter gains her strength, resilience, and wisdom. I used to think my job was to make things easier for her, to smooth the path ahead. But I've realized that it's more important to let her face challenges, to allow her the space to wrestle with her own problems.

For instance, my daughter has recently developed a fascination with sewing and crochet. At just nine years old, she amazes me with her creativity, designing and crafting clothing for her stuffed animals. Right now, she's diligently working on an apron from fabric we picked out together. I couldn't be prouder of her determination and her desire to learn these skills on her own.

I've learned that my role isn't to push or rush her learning but to offer her steady support and trust in her process. Every setback she faces is an opportunity for her to emerge stronger, and I've come to understand how vital it is to resist the urge to step in too quickly. By being patient and present, I've watched her find her own way, in her own time, becoming more capable than I ever could have imagined.

—

In patience, I find a disciplined space,
Where her creativity grows at its own pace.
She creates with fabric, glue, and thread;
In each little struggle, her confidence spreads.
I stand in awe as she finds her way,
In her own journey of growth, prouder every day.

—Sincerely, Boris

Maitri Blooms

Unconditional love involves cultivating loving-kindness toward ourselves and others, even during times of pain, suffering, or difficulty. Often, our habits of fear and avoidance block this love, but the key is to stay present with discomfort rather than seek escape or control. By doing so, we can soften and develop a compassion that extends to all beings. This approach helps dissolve the ego's need for security and deepens our connection to ourselves and the world.

—

In the heart's stillness,
a tender seed of maitri blooms,
unconditional and boundless.

In the present moment, free of grasping,
we touch the hearts of all beings,
where love, unbroken, endures.

—Sincerely, Boris

With A Little Help From Her Father

As I guide my daughter through the complexities of the world, I recognize that the pressures of modern culture seek to mold her in ways that may distort her sense of self. In this process, my role becomes one of fierce protection, gentle guidance, and deep listening.

I must first instill in her an unshakable belief in her intrinsic worth. Society will try to measure her by external standards—appearance, achievements, social validation—but I teach her that her value is inherent, stemming from her character, kindness, and the unique power she brings into the world. I show her that true confidence is cultivated from within, rooted in understanding who she is, rather than how others see her.

Part of this journey as a father is ensuring that she understands the importance of setting boundaries. I teach her to listen to her intuition and to assert herself, knowing that saying "no" is not a sign of weakness but of strength. In a culture that often exploits vulnerability, I help her discern trustworthiness in others and remind her that her body, her mind, and her heart are hers to protect (with a little help from her father).

It is essential that she finds a balance between independence and connection. I encourage her to pursue her passions with relentless curiosity while also fostering deep, meaningful relationships with those around her. The strength I want her to embody is not only about resilience in the face of challenges, but also about cultivating compassion for herself and others.

I embrace my role as a father in the fullness of my imperfections, showing her that strength is not about being infallible but about owning mistakes and learning from them. Through my actions, I seek to model what it means to be emotionally available and self-aware, to listen before responding, and to act with integrity.

As a divorced father, I have an added responsibility to provide her with stability, even when life feels fractured. I must be the steady presence in her life, offering her a safe haven where she can explore the world without fear of judgment. I make it clear to her that her family structure does not define her; she is not diminished by it, but can find strength in her ability to navigate its complexities with grace, as I have.

My love for her is an anchor, one that will carry her through the challenges of adolescence and beyond. My hope is that, through this unconditional love, she will grow into a woman who is not only strong but wise, empathetic, and unapologetically herself.

—

I promise, daughter, to be your guide,
To walk beside you, to never hide.
I'll show you strength and how to stand
With courage held in your own hand

I promise to let you grow and be,
To find your path and set you free.
In every step, through joy and strife,
I'll honor the woman you shape in life.

I promise to protect your heart,
To guard your spirit from the start.
No matter where I am or roam,
I'll always find my way back home.

—Sincerely, Boris

Trust Is A Slow Dance

Throughout my journey as a child and as an adult, I have come to realize that trust is not a simplistic or singular decision, but a process. It's not merely about extending trust to others, but about confronting my inner doubts, both about people and about the plan for my life. I've learned that my skepticism and reluctance to trust stem from wounds of the past, and from my fear of what might happen if I let go of control. Trust, I now see, isn't blind; it's informed by wisdom, discernment, and boundaries.

There were moments when I questioned not just others, but also the divine, wondering why painful experiences were allowed to happen, and why I was left feeling unprotected as a child and later in life as I grew into young adulthood. The uncertainty bred doubt in my own ability to discern who or what was safe. Yet what I have gained is an understanding that trust begins not with others, but with a foundational trust in a higher purpose, even when the path forward seems obscure.

I learned that trust is not something to be given indiscriminately or withheld entirely. It is an invitation to vulnerability, tempered by the understanding that discernment is a gift, honed through experience. It has become clear to me that trust is less about guarantees of safety or certainty and more about growth through relational and spiritual stretching. There is wisdom in establishing boundaries, not as a form of self-preservation, but as an act of respect for both myself and those around me. Boundaries do not signify the absence of trust, but rather the preservation of healthy, intentional trust.

The deepest lesson, however, is the recognition that trust requires a recalibration of my heart. It is not my role to control or to predict the actions of others or the unfolding of life's events, but to trust that each step I take, though uncertain, moves me closer to healing. I now understand that trust is a slow dance between wisdom and vulnerability, one that I must navigate with an open yet discerning heart. The fear that held me captive no longer defines my capacity to trust. Instead, trust becomes a daily practice of releasing control, setting healthy limits, and believing that I am safe within divine protection, even when circumstances remain unclear.

—

In childhood's darkest corners,
Fear lived behind the front door,
A silence I could not question
But learned not to trust.

Friends, once anchors,
Became driftwood in shallow waters,
Loyalty lost like whispers,
And I, abandoned, floating alone.

In a failed marriage, trust was a mirror
Shattered by pretense,
Each shard reflecting a version of myself
That I no longer recognized.

Relationships, at times, felt like betrayal,
A wound wrapped in promises,
Yet in moments of intimacy,
I found trust's delicate bloom.

Now, trust is a flickering light,
Sometimes dim, sometimes strong,
A compass not for others,
But for the faith I rebuild within myself.

—Sincerely, Boris

Embracing Transitions

As one season fades into the next, change mixes within us too, subtle yet profound. Just as the leaves turn from green to gold, the colors of our emotions shift with a perfect melody, answering the call of transformation. The world whispers its permission; it's okay to change. There is beauty in becoming.

We adapt to the crisp embrace of autumn, cocooned in layers that shield us from the coming chill. In this same rhythm, our desires and dreams transform; what we once yearned for dissolves like mist, giving way to new longings. Change is inevitable, but it's within these shifts that our hearts remain boundless, ever-hopeful for what's next: A future that evolves us.

Like the seasons, we watch those around us shed their old selves and grow into something new. There is beauty in witnessing that transformation, a privilege only life grants us. Hold close the memories of winter's past: The snowflakes that kissed our skin, the flowers that blossomed, the sun that warmed our bones, reminding us to carry its light through the seasons ahead.

Transitions are not just a passage, but a reflection of life's constancy; ever-shifting, ever-beautiful.

It is never too late to embrace change, no matter how deep our suffering or how lost we may feel. Life, with its relentless unpredictability, asks us to remain open, to face discomfort knowing that suffering is not an obstacle but an invitation to sit with discomfort, to be curious rather than fearful.

In moments of fear, confusion, and pain, there is quiet strength in patience. It is not about avoiding these feelings but softening into them, allowing ourselves to be vulnerable without retreat. The human spirit is not measured by how it escapes turmoil but by how it remains present in its depths.

Our inner turmoil is not a struggle to overcome but an experience to witness. Each moment of despair offers its own wisdom, and only through being fully present, holding it gently in our awareness, do we allow transformation to take place. Life asks us to be patient, to be kind to ourselves, and willing to remain in the experience, trusting that something meaningful is unfolding, even when all seems lost.

—

*We were young
and wanted to grow up.
But through the years,
you chased false dreams,
with me grounded in reality,
clinging on to hope.*

I paid for your rent,
the student loans, the credit cards,
the haircuts, the cell phones,
the groceries, the bank loans,
the transit, the clothes, the shoes,
the equipment, the tools, the ingredients,
the cars, the gas, the repairs,
the diapers, the toys, the books,
the tickets, the movies, the bills,
the breakfast, lunch, & dinners,
the furniture, the wedding, the home.

And in the end,
I also paid the price.

For I forgot to take care of
my heart,
my integrity,
my dignity,
my mind,
my body,
my soul,
my growth,
my health,
my self-worth,
myself entirely.

Now it's over.
I have less,
and you ask for more.

But in the end,
all I have left to offer
is forgiveness.

—Sincerely, Boris

Charting A Life Of Purpose and Clarity

For generations, men have been told to "suck it up", to bury their emotions in silence. Over time, this expectation hardened into a norm, leaving many numb, unable to summon the courage to become their truest selves and unlock their full potential. They traded sovereignty, inner leadership, and authentic masculinity for the fleeting comfort of external validation.

But beneath this stoic exterior lies an unspoken rejection of self, of vulnerability that has led many down the path of self-sabotage, anxiety, and quiet despair. When all along, the true liberation could be found in facing the emotions and patterns that keep them bound.

By embracing the inner work, men can chart a life of purpose and clarity, mastering the skills that nurture meaningful relationships and regulate mind, body, and soul. In this journey, they become fearless, not only for themselves but for the men, women, and children whose lives they touch.

I dream of a world where men are unafraid of vulnerability, where they seek healing from unhealthy pasts, shed old habits, and empower each other to break free from what holds them back. A world where they rise, not as prisoners of their pain, but as the best versions of themselves, leading with strength, grace, and love.

—

We were taught to quiet the heart,
To bury the ache and play the part,
To hold our tongues, to numb the pain,
And wear our strength like heavy chains.

But beneath the steel, beneath the stone,
A quiet storm calls us home.
Not to rage, not to deny,
But to feel, to rise, to ask why.

Why we hide from the tender light,
Why we fear the softer fight,
Why the weight of unshed tears
Becomes the armor of our years.

Yet in the cracks, a voice begins,
Whispering where true strength remains;
In the breaking, in the bend,
In the courage wounds can mend.

The path of grace is soft but sure,
Where love endures, where hearts mature.
Where men unlearn the myths of might,
And rise, with tenderness, to fight.

For in the fall, we find our wings;
In the stillness, healing sings.
The bravest heart, the clearest mind,
Is one that dares to feel, to find.

—Sincerely, Boris

Act Of Kindness

In my journey through life and career, I've learned that the foundation of meaningful success lies in the simplest yet most profound principles: Relentless effort and unwavering kindness. Each step up the corporate ladder, whether in media and advertising agencies or while climbing the ranks on the client side, has taught me that working hard is more than a matter of ambition; it's about resilience, consistency, and determination. Through every challenge, I've found that effort and integrity are what ultimately define progress.

Raising my daughter as a single father has deepened my understanding of the balance between effort and kindness. It's a constant reminder that perseverance isn't just about pushing through obstacles but also about creating a compassionate environment for others. Whether it's helping her with schoolwork, teaching her resilience, or simply being present, I've seen that the softer virtues of patience and empathy carry just as much weight as discipline and hard work.

In my career, I've had the privilege of serving on industry boards and contributing to conversations that shape the future of our work. Through it all, I've held onto the belief that success without kindness is empty. Kindness is not a weakness but a strength; it is the quiet force that builds trust, loyalty, and authentic relationships. In every meeting, in every collaboration, I strive to show kindness not as a tactic but as a way of living.

I've also realized that true success is not a solitary pursuit. It is enriched by the people around us; our colleagues, friends, and loved ones. Working in media agencies, leading teams, and driving growth has shown me that fostering an environment where people feel valued and respected yields better work, greater creativity, and lasting relationships.

In moments of professional triumph and personal reflection, I find myself drawn to the importance of being good to others, not because it's easy, but because it's essential. At the end of the day, our achievements may be measured by metrics, but our impact is measured by the way we make people feel. And so, I carry forward the simple truth that effort and kindness, together, are what shape not only careers but lives.

—

In the silence of winter's heavy snow,
where blankets shield and secrets grow,
two souls drift, bound by tender thread,
in whispered words, where few have tread.
Her gaze, a lantern bright,
guides him through the shroud of night.
In a world where faith and doubt collide,
She warms the parts he tries to hide.
Beneath the quilt's woven embrace,
They find a love both wild and chaste.
Through fragile glances, hands entwined,
they leave the past and faith behind.
But love, like snow, can swiftly fade,

its beauty brief, its mark still made.
As seasons shift, as distance grows,
their dreams dissolve in melting snow.
Yet in his heart, her voice remains;
a ghost of joy, a pulse of pain.
Through blankets thick and memories worn,
He carries love, forever torn.

—Sincerely, Boris

Story Time

When I talk about storytelling, it's more than just crafting a narrative; it's about capturing a piece of who you are and sharing it with the world. You have a story, and what makes it powerful is your ability to connect with others by being unapologetically yourself. The most compelling stories aren't those with grand plots, but those that come from a place of raw, personal truth. It's in your vulnerability that others will see themselves, and that's where real connection happens.

I've always had a deep passion for storytelling, whether it's in pop culture, advertising, media, or scripted content like books, films, music, theater, poetry, or even a presentation. These forms fascinate me because, at their core, they're all about how we communicate the human experience. Whether it's a commercial that moves you in thirty seconds or a film that lingers in your thoughts long after the credits roll, they all play with that delicate balance of revelation and restraint. Each medium has its own way of shaping a narrative, yet they all share that need to tap into something real and universal.

When you tell your story, don't focus on making it perfect. Focus on what it means to you. It doesn't need to be complex or intricate. Simplicity often carries more weight. What's important is that you convey the moments of change—the turning points that shaped your life. Those moments, no matter how small they may seem, carry within them a truth that others will resonate with. Your audience doesn't need to be wowed by spectacle; they need to be moved by the humanity in your story. And this is what I strive for in my personal and professional projects.

And remember, your perspective is unique. It's your voice that makes your story worth listening to. Whether you're writing a book, directing a film, or sharing your personal journey with a friend (or to the entire world), you have the ability to touch others. It's not just about sharing your experiences; it's about inviting others to see the world in a new way through your eyes. That's what storytelling is for me: A way to show people something they might not have noticed before, a way to connect us all through our shared human experience.

When you speak your truth, and you do it with purpose, the world listens. That's the power of storytelling. And every time you tell your story, you'll learn a little more about yourself in the process.

—

I write in silence, letters like whispers,
to a world I am unable to connect with.
I sit here at the edge of it all,
feeling way too much, saying far too little.

Then she arrived, with her eyes like a portal to a better place. They pulled me in; into music, into nights that stretched forever, into the kind of living I thought I'd only ever watch in movies or read in books.

And there we were, wrapped in the warmth of shared secrets, and I knew, in that moment, we were forever.

But infinity has its darkness.
I watched as pain hid behind familiar smiles.
And I realized that love, in all its beauty,
is never quite as simple as it seems.

Life is a tapestry woven with threads of acceptance, where those who blossom in kindness thrive, and those ignored or mistreated carry the weight of silence.

Each story, a reflection of who we are;
each moment, a call for understanding,
reminding us that the heart finds light
in the embrace of those who truly see.

Memories resurfaced once more, dark and quiet, pulling me back to places I'd tried to forget. In the end, I came to understand the quiet truth: we accept the things we feel we deserve.

—Sincerely, Boris

The Moment I Knew (It Was Over)

In this moment, I find myself at a crossroads, reflecting on the journey that has led me here. The end of a relationship is never just an event; it is a process of untangling oneself from shared dreams, plans, and the hope of a future once imagined. I have learned that loss, as painful as it may be, is not the end but a doorway; one that opens to the possibility of growth, of rediscovering who I am outside the bounds of another.

Letting go, truly releasing, is an act of strength, not weakness. It means accepting that I cannot control the actions or emotions of others, but I can control my response to the situation. It means accepting the reality as it is, not as I wished it would be. I've come to understand that self-worth does not hinge on the validation or approval of another. It is something I cultivate within myself, built from a foundation of resilience, honesty, and self-respect. I must stand in the fullness of my own value, and that takes courage.

What I have endured, both in the toxicity of my past marriage and the recent heartbreak with my girlfriend, has shown me the necessity of boundaries. Boundaries are not walls to keep others out but lines drawn to protect my emotional and mental well-being. They allow me to engage with others while maintaining my own sense of identity and purpose. Through this experience, I have learned to listen more attentively to my instincts, to recognize red flags, and to honor my needs without shame or apology.

As a father, I realize that the way I move through this pain, the way I choose to rebuild, is not just for me but for my daughter as well. She is watching, learning from my actions. I want to show her that it's possible to grieve and still move forward, to embrace the lessons of loss and emerge stronger on the other side. It's a painful process, but one that is necessary for growth, for becoming the person I am meant to be.

In the quiet spaces of reflection, I have learned that healing is not linear. There are days of progress, and days where the weight of the past presses heavily on my chest. But each day, I make the choice to rise, to rebuild, to step into the unknown with trust in myself. I no longer look for closure in others; I find it within. This is where my power lies: Knowing that I have survived, that I can thrive even in the absence of what I once held dear.

Ultimately, this is about reclaiming my life, my joy, and my peace. It's about rewriting my story, one where I am the protagonist who, despite the scars of the past, stands tall and moves forward, not in bitterness, but in hope.

–

When I heard you say
You were falling in love
With him and not me,
That was the moment I knew
It was over.

Your gentle words,
Softly spoken, with hesitancy,
Understood the pain I would feel,
Shouted at me,
Clearly and unintentionally loud.

Stop trying,
Stop fighting,
Stop reaching,
Stop holding on.
It's over.

Just stop, and let you go.
As you have done with me.
That was the moment I knew
It was really over.

—Sincerely, Boris

Having You By My Side

Raising a daughter has been an unparalleled journey of learning, reflection, and growth. Through the stories of others, I've found wisdom that resonates with the deep responsibility and profound love that comes with being a father to my beautiful daughter. One of the greatest lessons I have embraced is that fatherhood is not about control but about nurturing independence. It's about standing alongside her as she explores the world, offering guidance when she seeks it, and always making sure she knows that my love is her safe place, no matter where life leads her.

I've also learned that my role is to model emotional vulnerability. To show her that strength is not in silence, but in expressing her thoughts and feelings with clarity and confidence. This is especially important in a world that often tries to diminish the emotional depth of girls, pushing them to conform to shallow expectations. I want her to understand that her feelings matter, that she is not only allowed to take up space but encouraged to do so fully and unapologetically.

Patience, too, has revealed itself as a critical virtue. I've realized that our time together isn't always about monumental moments but is instead composed of the quiet, steady presence I offer her. She doesn't need me to be perfect; she needs me to be present. In those small, everyday interactions—the mundane conversations on our walks and on the swing sets, the shared laughter over a meal or movie—our bond grows, and so does her understanding of what a loving relationship looks like.

Finally, I've come to appreciate that teaching her resilience is perhaps my greatest duty. Not the kind of resilience that hardens, but the kind that allows her to rise after each fall with grace and strength. I want her to know that failure is never final, that setbacks are simply stepping stones, and that her worth is never defined by the obstacles she encounters. It is in her ability to rise, to face the world with compassion for herself and others, that she will find her true power.

As a single father, I strive to be the kind of man who mirrors these values; not just for her sake, but for my own growth, too. Fatherhood is not a journey with a clear destination but a continuous process of becoming. I know that as I guide her, she is guiding me, both of us evolving together in this shared, sacred relationship.

—

I once believed my strength was my own,
Built through hardship and endurance.
But in you, I've realized,
It's your presence that keeps me moving forward.

In your laughter, I find hope,
And in your compassion, I understand
That kindness is where real strength lies.
You may be young, but you guide me,
Teaching lessons I didn't know I needed.

You've shown me how to listen,
How to stay patient, and how to nurture growth.
Your resilience is clear in every challenge you face;
You get back up without hesitation.

I'm proud of how independent you've become,
Of the way you meet life head-on.
Watching you grow into your own
Is the greatest gift I could have.

You've given me strength I never thought I'd need,
And I'm better for having you by my side.

—Sincerely, Boris

I hear the birds singing & leaves rustling.
I see green grass & the blue sky.
I smell flowers & fresh air.
I taste ice cream & freezies.
I touch the sand & grass.

—Sincerely, Macy

(Self) Love Is A Choice

Love, in all its varied forms, has shaped me. It is through love that I have discovered the complexities of friendship, the exhilaration and heartache of romance, and the beauty of self-discovery. The years have taught me that love is not confined to the romantic ideals we often hold in our youth, but rather, it permeates every facet of life; friendship, family, and, perhaps most importantly, the love we cultivate within ourselves.

Through friendships, I learned the art of companionship, the silent language of loyalty, and the sharp pain of betrayal. Friends are the scaffolding upon which the architecture of my life has been built, and though time may weather those bonds, I understand now that each connection serves its purpose, either to uplift or to teach.

Romantic love, for all its allure, often presents itself as a mirror reflecting back our deepest insecurities and desires. It is within the pursuit of love that I have faltered, my heart at times shattered by misplaced trust or unfulfilled promises. Yet I have come to see that the true tragedy of love is not its ending, but the missed opportunities to grow alongside someone who enriches you, rather than diminishes you.

In the midst of seeking external validation, I realized that the most profound relationship is the one I have with myself. Self-love, often overlooked, is the foundation upon which all other forms of love must be built. It is in moments of solitude that I have found clarity, understanding that I must first learn to stand alone before I can truly stand with others.

Life's most valuable lessons are delivered not in grand epiphanies, but in the quiet moments; through friendships that evolve, through relationships that end, and through the resilience we muster in solitude. What remains is the awareness that love, in its many forms, is less about perfect outcomes and more about the journey—the vulnerability, the joy, and the inevitable pain that accompanies it.

Each encounter, whether fleeting or enduring, has etched itself into the fabric of who I am. And from this, I have learned that love, above all else, is a choice, one we must make with grace, courage, and perhaps most of all, with a deep sense of compassion for ourselves.

—

Before I stand with you,
I must stand with myself
In quiet corners of solitude,
Where no hand holds mine,
And no voice echoes back my worth.

I must be whole,
Not seeking refuge in another's eyes,
But rooted in the soil of my own soul,
Blooming from the love I give within.

Only then,
With steady hands and open heart,
Can I walk beside you,
Not as half seeking whole,
But as one who knows how to love
By first loving myself.

—Sincerely, Boris

The Purest Form Of Grace And
The Promise Of Something More

I've come to understand that detachment is not abandonment but rather an act of self-respect; a quiet declaration that I deserve peace, that I refuse to be bound by cycles of unreciprocated love or relentless strain.

For fourteen years, I tried to keep a relationship alive, mistaking resilience for staying power. I worked tirelessly, and my world narrowed to appeasing, to soothing, to holding on when there was nothing left to hold. I learned how to accept silence where there should've been comfort, slept on the floor while trying to sustain what we built together. I lost my sense of worth to a hope that maybe one day, things might change. It took years to see that love shouldn't be a negotiation, and that the best loyalty is sometimes to oneself.

Stepping away was painful, and the act of never looking back demanded a kind of courage I hadn't tapped into before. But there's a quiet power in leaving with grace. I've learned that not every path is meant to be traveled forever, and sometimes we honor love most by letting it go.

Recently, I faced this lesson again, standing on the edge of possibility with someone I loved deeply. I wanted so badly to bridge the gap, to bring her back. But in this journey, I've realized that love, true love, chooses you back. It should stand beside you, as unwavering as your own will.

So I stepped back, choosing myself over chasing what wasn't reaching for me anymore.

In these moments, I teach my daughter what it means to walk away with dignity. I hope she sees that choosing herself will never be a weakness, but an understanding that we should always honor our own values. We deserve someone who sees the worth in the effort we give, someone who meets us where we are. And until that person comes along, we have our own strength to lean on.

What this has taught me is that walking away isn't an ending; it's making space for something better. It's trusting that when we let go of what harms us, we open the door to what can truly fill us. And above all, I want my daughter to remember: Walking away is not a failure; it's the purest form of grace, an affirmation of our worth, and the promise of something more.

—

He did not surrender,
but chose a gentler path;
not out of weakness,
but the strength to finally let go.

He gave her his heart and soul,
filled the empty spaces with care,
held onto hope for a second chance,
for love and future with patience
until it slipped away.

In the clarity of distance,
he saw the truth he'd hidden from:
that sometimes love must loosen its grip,
not to vanish, but to be set free.

So he walked away,
not bitter, nor broken,
but with the grace of a man who knows
that peace and respect weigh more
than a love that no longer reaches back.

And though he carries the sadness,
he feels the weight lifting;
his own quiet redemption,
a testament to the heart
that could have held on forever
but chose instead
to walk forward.

—Sincerely, Boris

Colours Of Life

In my journey through the depths of human emotion, I have come to understand the necessity of embracing the full spectrum of feelings. I have learned that to truly live, I must allow myself to feel every emotion, without judgment or resistance. There is no hierarchy of feelings; joy, sadness, fear, and pleasure are all woven into the fabric of my being. To reject any part of this tapestry is to reject a part of myself.

Through this reflection, I see that emotional wholeness is not the absence of pain but the willingness to meet it with compassion. When I honor the discomforts that arise, I am granted deeper access to the richness of life, and it is here that I find meaning. Avoiding pain may offer temporary relief, but it denies me the opportunity to grow and evolve.

This path requires vulnerability, an openness not only with others but with myself. I must release the need for control and certainty, accepting that uncertainty and imperfection are intrinsic to human existence. By surrendering to this truth, I find the freedom to be authentic, present, and fully engaged with the world.

In relationships, I realize that emotional intimacy flourishes when both individuals can sit with their own feelings and, by extension, hold space for the feelings of others. The bonds I seek are forged not through avoiding discomfort but through the courage to be seen as I am, in both light and darkness within me.

I have come to understand that emotions are guides, not enemies. They are here to teach me, to lead me toward deeper understanding, connection, and transformation. It is through feeling it all, without numbing, without denial, that I find true liberation.

—

Each emotion has its space,
each one part of what makes us human.
I carry them all,
not as weight,
but as the colors of life.

In feeling them, I find peace;
not by pushing them away,
but by living through each one.

Sincerely, Boris

Forging Grit

In my journey as a marketer and strategist, working within the dynamic world of media and advertising, I've come to realize that success is not born from flashes of creative brilliance alone. It is something deeper, a persistent force—grit—that has driven my professional development and growth. It has become clear to me that in an industry where innovation, creativity, and strategy is highly valued, it's not enough to simply have vision. Sustaining that vision requires dedication, discipline, and the ability to weather setbacks with unwavering resolve.

Early in my career, I believed that raw talent or the next big idea would be the key to success. But with time, I came to see that ideas, much like passion, are fleeting unless coupled with a dogged commitment to execution. Campaigns aren't made great by the initial spark of inspiration; they succeed through relentless iteration, feedback, and optimization. It's not the glamour of pitching an idea that creates long-term impact; it's the persistence in refining it, over and over, even when the outcome isn't immediately clear.

I've learned that in media and advertising, failure is inevitable. Campaigns don't always hit the mark, trends shift, and audiences are ever-evolving. But rather than being discouraged by setbacks, I've grown to view them as critical moments in my professional development. Each challenge, whether it's a missed opportunity or a campaign that falls short, has become a lesson in resilience. With each, I've honed my ability to pivot, to absorb feedback, and to adapt, skills that are as essential as creativity in this fast-paced industry.

In the same way that grit shapes personal success, it's the cornerstone of professional growth in media. Success is less about having one breakthrough moment and more about showing up every day with determination, ready to push forward despite the obstacles. I've seen how those who persist, who learn from failure, and who continuously strive for improvement in their craft are the ones who ultimately thrive.

As I reflect on my career, I understand now that it wasn't my initial creative spark that defined my trajectory, but my willingness to grind through the mundane aspects of the process, to work toward long-term goals even when progress was slow. It's this fusion of passion and perseverance that has allowed me to turn ideas into impactful campaigns, and to evolve in an ever-changing industry.

—

It's not the spark that lights the flame,
But steady hands, day after day.
A mind that bends but will not break,
Through every challenge, for progress' sake.

It's not in speed, nor strength, nor flight,
But rising up, time after time.
For grit is forged in quiet strain,
A constant push against the grain.

When all seems lost, and dreams grow dim,
Grit finds the strength to try again.

—Sincerely, Boris

Moments Of Singular Presence

I have met a woman who captivates my curiosity in ways that are both subtle and sincere. She possesses an enchanting smile, one that invites contemplation, and her intellect is a reservoir of knowledge.

Our time together began in simplicity, which brought with it the slow transition from casual exchanges to more intimate encounters. It was just the two of us, seated beside one another at her wooden dining table—an otherwise unremarkable place transformed into the locus of a quiet, passionate moment. There, amidst the remnants of earlier conversations and the subtle hush of the night, we began to truly reveal ourselves, not merely through the words exchanged but through the silences that punctuated them.

Our questions, though innocuous at first, grew longer in their responses, drawing us closer, as though the very chairs we occupied were conspiring to bring our bodies nearer. And in time, they did. The space between us vanished, until we found ourselves no longer seated apart but sharing an almost singular presence.

In that instant, as if time itself paused in reverence, our lips met. The kiss was neither hurried nor fleeting, but rather the kind that stretches across the span of hours. Our hands explored, tracing paths not unlike the threads of our earlier conversations; each touch unveiled a new dimension of understanding, as if we were learning each other in a language foreign yet familiar. It was as if our bodies communicated where words could not, translating the intrigue of thought into something palpable and electric.

-

As we sit under the autumn sun,
Our knees brush the earth,
Your eyes trace soft paths between us.

Our children play in the distance,
Their laughter singing a song we both know well.

Between bites of a shared sandwich,
We exchange stories,
Untangling the past and present
Until we begin to speak of dreams
We had both long forgotten.

In the stillness between breaths,
My hand finds your leg;
Before our children return,
You steal a kiss, quick as a secret.
I smile, and steal it back.

When our children return to the picnic,
Their hands full of discoveries,
We sit, caught in the moment's pause;
No longer stealing kisses,
But sharing them softly,
As if they belong only to us.

—Sincerely, Boris

Celestial Being

Beneath the midnight canvas of the night,
My fingers trace the arc of the stars above;
their gentle glow recall the shape of you,
as if the sky mirrored your elegant grace.

Orion rises, bold and timeless,
its figure echoing your silhouette,
an hourglass carved by light and shadow,
each star a freckle, a scar, a wrinkle of time.

I let my fingers slowly drift,
connecting these celestial points,
as if by touch I might reveal
the world's most sacred design;
your beauty woven among the stars.

And though the sky holds you just beyond my reach,
still I trace, mapping your constellation,
forever etched in the motion of the cosmos,
where even distance cannot dim the shine of your light.

—Sincerely, Boris

Face The Fear

In depths so deep, where fears are found,
We seek the space to not be bound,
But suffering, like winds that blow,
Will follow us where we want to go.

To grasp for calm, to turn away,
Leaves us lost in disarray.
The need to flee, to dull the pain,
Is what keeps us dry from the rain.

But in the storm, if we all stand still,
And let the pain do as it will,
It fades like mist before the dawn,
And soon its weight is fully gone.

So face the fear, and do not flee;
In presence lies tranquility.
For in this moment, if we stay,
We find our peace won't slip away.

Let the sun, shine through the fear,
To grow our seed we planted here.
For today and everyday,
All our fears will go away.

—Sincerely, Boris

Good Morning

I wake while the world rests in silence,
tiptoeing past your peaceful dreams.
The coffee's warmth fills the early light,
toast browning, eggs softly cooking,
and bacon crackling as the day begins.

I lean in to kiss your cheek,
captivated by how morning softens your face.
Another kiss, and you stretch,
holding onto me for more,
drawing me closer into the comfort of the morning.

In these quiet moments, time slows,
our whispers soft, breaths mingling
as we savor the closeness,
wrapped around each other, indulging in tender kisses,
lost in each other before the world beckons.

Steam rises from our cups,
filling the room with warmth as light spills in,
each moment deepening with shared laughter
and the simple joy of breakfast together.

We gather as the morning unfolds,
and with one final kiss, I send you into the day,
knowing it begins with the touch of our lips,
the taste of simple joy.

—Sincerely, Boris

Making Space For The Possibility Of Love

The beauty of meeting someone new lies in the untold stories they carry—chapters written before your existence. You listen with quiet wonder, hanging onto each word, as their past unfolds like a secret view through a window, distant yet inviting.

The magic is in creating your own firsts; moments stitched together in memory, woven into stories you'll both tell, shared laughter between friends and family, retold with love.

There's a privilege in unlocking their mind, tracing the intricate paths where emotions and actions meet, discovering the quiet beauty of how they think, how they feel.

Exploration, too, is slow and deliberate, every inch of them drawing you closer, deeper, until what's left to discover resides inside, where the real journey begins. And there's hope in meeting their loved ones, hoping that one day you'll be counted among them.

But perhaps the most thrilling part is the optimism. The way your heart begins to shift, making space for the possibility of love, knowing that this journey was never meant to be walked alone; it's a road for two.

–

I am taken away, not just by your beauty
But by the essence in which you carry it,
So effortlessly as if it was weightless.
Each moment a harmony of elements,
Transcending the surface to touch the soul.

I am taken away, not only by your growth,
But by the way you've nurtured it;
Through nourishment and sunlight.
Each moment a testament to your self-care,
Transforming you into your full potential.

Take me along with you,
Until I've been completely
Taken away by you.

—Sincerely, Boris

Truest Mark Of Love

Sometimes, life comes down to the things left unsaid, the choices we once couldn't make, or the words we were too afraid to say. I've thought about this deeply, especially with the echoes of my last relationship, where love became something shared with my daughter, too. Watching them together stirred something new in me, something that felt both tender and weighted, knowing how close we all were and the emotions that had layered over time.

In love and life, I've realized, timing is as much an enemy as it is a friend. There are relationships you hold in your heart long after they're gone, because in some way, they're stitched into who you are. Letting go, I learned, doesn't mean forgetting. It means honoring what it gave you, allowing yourself to grow around the loss and the memories alike. And part of that growth, for me, has been opening up to my daughter, showing her the sides of love that endure; friendship, loyalty, and the courage to embrace life's impermanence without resentment.

There's a quiet strength in moving forward, I think, but it also means having the patience to live with what's unresolved. Sometimes, the most meaningful connections leave us with loose ends. In those gaps between what we once shared and what remains, I try to find peace; not just for myself, but for the kind of man, father, and friend I want to be. And that, I've learned, might be the truest mark of love.

—

In the meadows of my daughter's laughter,
she found a friend, a mentor, a guide;
a woman who spoke to the world as if every leaf and feather
carried a secret worth holding close.

I'd watch them both, fingers intertwined,
two souls bound in wonder,
eyes wide with the shared love of nature's beauty.

They made gifts from paper and glue,
sketched treasures and braided wishes into chests full of
memories,
as if they, together, could grow a world all their own.

She became more than love,
more than a hand to hold beside mine;
she was someone I'd have proudly called partner,
shoulder to shoulder, raising my daughter with honor.

But that world we dreamt, its warmth and wild simplicity,
is gone now, fading like the sunset that lit their sky.
I look at my daughter and see traces of her curiosity,
the way they shared secrets I will miss greatly.

It is the saddest truth I carry;
to love what's gone, and to walk forward in its dissolve.
Yet for the bond they wove so carefully, so tenderly,
I am forever grateful, and forever grieving.

—Sincerely, Boris

Poem Of The Dead

As I navigate through life, I am increasingly aware of the deep connection between living and dying. Each moment serves as a reminder that everything is temporary, urging me to seek the truths within myself.

Facing the possibility of death due to two brain aneurysms was a turning point for me. The thought of having only a one-third chance of surviving surgery forced me to confront my fears directly. I realized that death is not merely an ending; it can also be a gateway to something new. This experience opened my eyes to the importance of embracing every moment and the love I share with those around me.

During my recovery, I reflected on my life in a way I never had before. I encountered vivid memories and emotions that mirrored my thoughts and actions, revealing the depth of my journey. I learned that dying is a transition, a sacred opportunity for change. With each breath, I strive to cultivate awareness and find clarity amid the noise and chaos.

I began to appreciate love and compassion more than ever, understanding that these feelings connect me to everyone else. My actions impact the world around me, emphasizing our shared existence.

I am learning to accept that life and death are part of a continuous cycle, a journey of growth and renewal. By accepting this flow, I have opened myself to new possibilities and deeper understanding. I have found peace in the realization that, despite the uncertainties, life is a precious gift that I cherish every day.

—

In the quiet of the mind, I find clarity,
Life and death intertwined, both a single path.
In the bardo, I encounter my fears;
Illusions dissolve as awareness arises.

Compassion guides me through the unknown;
Love transcends the boundaries of self.
Each moment is a lesson in letting go.
Embracing impermanence, I find freedom.

As I awaken, I see the cycle of rebirth;
In every ending, a new beginning unfolds.
With each breath, I cultivate presence,
And in stillness, I connect with all that is.

—Sincerely, Boris

Embracing (People) Change

In the quiet aftermath of our parting, I began to understand the real meaning of change; not as a loss, but as a natural evolution that neither of us could hold back. Our relationship was once built on connection, a shared path that felt unwavering. But over time, I realized that love alone couldn't prevent us from becoming people neither of us had anticipated.

She and I grew, but not always in the same direction. Where I once held onto the idea of us growing old together, I now see the wisdom in embracing how we each changed. My last relationship became a mirror, reflecting not just who I was with her, but who I was becoming alone. In seeing her change, I had to accept my own transformation, too. Letting go wasn't a failure; it was an act of grace, of allowing each of us to be whole without trying to force the pieces back together.

Walking away felt like shedding a weight, like letting go of a version of myself I no longer needed. I thought I was holding onto love, but in reality, I was holding onto a memory of us, a friendship we never truly built, even though we once shared so much. We were strangers with a past, familiar faces drifting into separate futures.

Change has never come easily to me, but now I see there's beauty in it: A chance to honor what we shared and to embrace who I am becoming. I walk forward, free of the illusion that we could keep everything the same. To change is to surrender to life's quiet, ceaseless transformations, and I am grateful to carry that lesson forward.

—

Today, I close a door left open wide
But never locked, in case one day, you seek
To return to the place we called our own,
A space once shared, now distant yet near.

On my side, memories linger, healing
From the bond we nurtured, fragile yet full;
But missing still, a knock from the other side,
A sign that you remember, too.

On your side, your hand lingers on the handle,
Hesitant, unsure if the past is worth revisiting,
Afraid it may remind you of a love once tender,
That slipped through our fingers like sand.

Our hands meet; two souls on opposite sides,
Turning the knob together,
Opening the door once more.
What begins as a polite greeting
Melds into an embrace,
A hug that stretches time,
Filling the air with memories.

We are carried back
To a time when we stood on the same side of the door,
Happy, united, alive in our shared warmth.
We leave it unlocked,
For whatever future may come.

A door is just a door;
And though we close it now,
It will never be locked,
For the love and friendship we once knew
Still lingers, waiting, on both sides.

So with a breath, he let her go,
Released the final tie,
And in the silence, he'd come to know
It was his last goodbye.

—Sincerely, Boris

An Easy Pill To Swallow

In the recent months, I have been reflecting on letting go of someone I loved deeply and the ways in which it has been both a challenge and a gift. Though we didn't share a long history, our connection felt like a rare, enduring bond that had felt like a lifetime of passion and care. In that brief time, I felt truly seen and accepted in a way that gave me hope, as if a new world had opened. Now, in releasing that dream, I've come to see that each relationship, whether brief or lasting, has shaped my understanding of how I wish to love and be loved.

Throughout my dating journey, I've met incredible people. Each connection has offered unique lessons, insights, and reflections of who I am and who I want to become. There's a richness to those experiences, even when they don't lead to lasting partnership. They remind me of the qualities I admire in others and in myself; the qualities that, with time, will align in a way that feels right. Rather than giving up on finding love, I see these relationships as part of a continuous journey that strengthens my vision of the life and love I want to create.

The more I've grown, the clearer I've become on the ways I want to give and receive love. I'm learning that love, at its best, feels like a balance of freedom and presence, moments of vulnerability and self-respect. As I move forward, I'm more intentional about what I want from a partner; qualities that foster a sense of mutual respect, shared values, and an unspoken understanding. My experiences have shown me that love thrives not when it's forced or pursued out of fear, but when it's nurtured from a place of genuine connection and trust.

Letting go of a deep love has brought me closer to my purpose, reminded me of my strength, and deepened my faith in the journey. Moving forward doesn't mean leaving behind the beauty of what we shared; instead, I carry it with me, allowing it to fuel my hope for the future. I honor what was, release it with love, and step forward with renewed clarity. This journey is far from over; I remain open, curious, and hopeful, trusting that each new connection will bring me closer to a love that feels like home.

—

Heartbreak, a bitter medicine,
teaches me where I ache and why,
where I bend and where I break,
where I must learn to stand alone.

In each loss, a deeper knowing,
a softening to love's open arms,
and the courage to seek,
again and again,
a love that feels like home.

—Sincerely, Boris

Conversations In Dating

Her: *Do you ever travel?*
Him: *I travel around the sun once a year.*

—Sincerely, Boris

My Craft: An Aspiring Innovator

In the world of media and advertising, creating for impact demands an intuitive alignment between concept and medium. This work showed me the importance of ideation that is both fluid and grounded, where ideas evolve to fit each medium's distinct character, yet still carry the brand's essence and purpose. I've come to realize that powerful design isn't merely about aesthetics but about the resonance it creates. Each campaign reminded me that concepts are the true connective tissue across platforms; they require rigor in thought yet the flexibility to adapt across touchpoints.

Stewarding clients' investments is a responsibility that runs deep in this process, requiring constant exploration and innovation to maximize reach, relevance, and return. Each activation must be crafted with a dual focus: Pushing the boundaries of creative possibility while ensuring alignment with the brand's core purpose and audience relevance. This is where uncovering new insights becomes indispensable. Understanding the audience, often through patterns hidden in data or trends just starting to emerge, is what fuels a campaign's strength and longevity. It's not just about meeting current needs but anticipating future desires and connecting brands to audiences in ways that feel fresh, authentic, and timely.

Over the last twenty years as a marketer and strategist, there's a lesson I keep returning to: Ideas are alive; they breathe through the collective experiences of creators and audiences alike. Balancing the tangible, budgetary demands of a project with the abstract desire for human connection is an art that transcends the numbers and metrics. Every media buy, every placement, every visual was more than its immediate return on investment (ROI). It's a statement, a subtle promise that targeted audiences would feel seen, understood, and even inspired.

This approach to media and advertising isn't purely technical; it's deeply philosophical. It's about holding space for ideas to manifest uniquely within the constraints of each medium or platform. In my work with major holding companies and on industry boards, I've learned that industry standards must often bow to innovation; that breaking conventions thoughtfully is where the magic lies.

—

In metrics, trends, where data leads,
We shape ideas from audience needs.
Algorithms hum; insights are clear;
As the story unfolds, direction appears.

Past rules dissolve, conventions fade;
A shift, a spark, a mark remade.

—Sincerely, Boris

Trips Around the Sun

There is no better time than now to pause, to look back, and to honor the path that has brought me here.

For many years, I wandered, lost, weighed down by a life that no longer made sense, a life that felt distant from my own heart. But in the last four years, I began the journey of reclaiming my happiness, a happiness rooted in putting myself first; nurturing my mind, body, spirit, and the love I share with my daughter.

In these years of transformation, I have emerged from a toxic, soul-wounding marriage. I've endured the loss of an eye, now replaced by a prosthetic, and faced the shadow of two brain aneurysms.

Through it all, I held fast to hope, knowing that even in uncertainty, beauty could still flourish. Moments of falling in and out of love, of laughter shared with friends around a table, of travels that opened my spirit, and of watching my daughter bloom before my eyes—all remind me that life is an intricate dance of joy and hardship. Every lesson, every tear, every triumph is a gift I will one day pass to her.

And now, as I stand in the present moment, I am overwhelmed by gratitude; grateful to still be here, breathing, surrounded by the ones I hold dear.

As I begin another journey around the sun, I offer these words to myself and to anyone who finds them:

1. Happiness is here, now, in the present. In this moment of reflection, I am filled with joy, and I wish the same for all who read this.

2. Cherish each breath. Let meditation be your guide. In the simple act of breathing in and out, we find our way back to ourselves, to the present where life unfolds.

3. The world can be dark and frightening, but awareness opens the path to light. By staying mindful of the problems facing our planet, we can respond with compassion, knowing how to help and when to protect.

Practice mindfulness in each passing moment. In doing so, we cultivate peace, within ourselves and for others. Be a protector of peace, for yourself and for those in need.

So, with this next journey, I make a promise to myself: I will embrace the present with open arms. I will let the sun's warmth rest on my skin more often. I will read more beautiful words, love more deeply, and savor every precious moment that this life gifts me.

—Sincerely, Boris

The Perfect Teacher

*In this very moment, the perfect teacher shares wisdom;
not in the comfort of certainty, but in the ache of
uncertainty.*

*We feel a force calling us to remain present,
to lean into what we'd rather escape,
which is the easier route we often gravitate towards.*

*Pain, discomfort, the rawness of being;
each one a doorway to growth, each one urging us to soften,
to open our hearts wider than we have before.*

*To run away from fear is to miss the lesson;
To stay is to cultivate and embrace compassion.*

*Vulnerability is not a weakness but the path to wisdom;
for within the cracks of our being, we can invite the light
inside ourselves.*

*This moment, this fleeting, fragile moment, holds
everything we need; if only we dare to really listen, to really
embrace, and to really be.*

*In accepting the chaos in the outside world,
we find our truest selves, and through it,
We learn to love not only ourselves but everyone else, too.*

—Sincerely, Boris

Closure

I let my fear of happiness steal away my chance to share a life with you. In doing so, I left you to choose another path, and I don't fault you for it. I've become a fleeting figure in your life, and while the chance to reclaim that closeness feels lost, I hold space for the unknown. Should our paths ever realign, I will fiercely hold onto the love I once shielded, speaking the truths I left unspoken.

I now know, with unwavering certainty, that I wanted to grow old with you; to create a family, a home. Your bond with children, so gentle and intuitive, made my heart gravitate toward you even more. I could see us as a family, with my child adoring you as I do. I was comforted by the idea of you becoming more than a cherished partner, but a co-parent, a confidante. I've always admired your natural grace in difficult moments, something that only deepened my trust.

I dreamed of standing beside you, shoulder-to-shoulder, raising my child not just as a father, but as partners, equals, sharing the weight of life's joys and burdens. The loss of that dream cuts deep, perhaps the most painful wound in this chapter of my life. I was starting to become very comfortable with the idea of you becoming more connected as a family. I would have been proud if you had one day stood by my side, shoulder-to-shoulder, as an equal, raising my child as my partner and as your own.

I regret the walls I built, the way I shut you out when you were offering your love. In my fear, I left you vulnerable and heartbroken. In my absence, another now holds the space I once occupied. I am left with guilt for what I couldn't give and sorrow for what I lost.

I deeply apologize for the hurt, frustration, and confusion I caused, both during and after our time together. Hurting you was never my intention. You made me feel like I was the only one that mattered. In return, I never imagined it would end like this; me, taking away the future we had once started mapping out together.

Letting go of you, of the life we could have shared, is a daily ache. I am confronted with the reality that you have moved on; your heart no longer holds mine. You've asked for distance, for no contact, and I have faltered in respecting that. It fills me with shame and remorse. The trust we had has crumbled, and we are unsure how to be even friends now. This, too, weighs on me.

But in knowing you, I've learned a deeper love and a clearer sense of self. Heartbreak has reshaped me, and I welcome that transformation. I am learning to heal, through reading, writing, and meditation, and this journey, though painful, is for me. It's a journey toward healing, for the sake of my future and for my child's.

I give myself permission to grieve the loss of you, to mourn not only our love but the friendship that once flourished between us. But I promise to use this sorrow as fuel for growth. I won't close the door on love, not for me, and not for my child. We both deserve joy and connection.

Therapy calls me back, not as a way to reconcile with you, but to reconcile with myself. It was once my grounding force, and I need that anchor again. One day, when the time is right, I hope to thank you for the hope you brought me after my surgery; not as a lover, but perhaps as a friend.

I'm closing this chapter, not in bitterness, but in grace. One day, your memory will be less of a lingering ache, and more of a distant, beautiful reminder of what I once held dear. I move forward with love still tucked quietly within me, not as a weight, but as a reminder of what I've known, learned, and become.

The impact you've had on my life cannot be overstated, and the reflections I'm left with are profound. This heartbreak, though painful, has opened doors to self-understanding, teaching me the depths of love, trust, and vulnerability. I honor this pain, and I honor the joy we shared. I commit to my healing, to my child, and to a future where love finds me again—where I show up as the father, partner, and man I am destined to be.

-

Like every tale, ours met its close—
Not the ending I had chosen.
No friendship left, just distant ties;
We've changed too much beneath the skies.

It wasn't for lack of care or try,
But time moved on, and so did I.
No more love, no joyful sound,
Just silence where we once were bound.

I lay to rest the dreams we knew,
The possibilities we had both clung onto.
The final page it now must turn;
Individually, we have much to learn.

And as we close this book with grace,
We say goodbye and find our place.
Some things in life just aren't meant to be,
And that's a lesson that you have taught me.

—Sincerely, Boris

The Hardest Things I've Had to Say

Today, I realized I'm no longer in love with you;
It was the memories, not the person, that stayed true.
For the first time in a long time, I woke up free,
Not caring if you messaged back, not fearing what I'd see.

The truth is, you're no longer the one I once knew;
That voice, that face, it's faded, too.
Time apart, while mending my heart,
Forced me to see how far we've grown apart.

This morning, it hit me deep and clear;
I'm no longer in love with you, my dear.
For the first time in a long time, I don't long for your touch;
You've become someone I don't recognize as much.

Perhaps it's for the best, this change I now face;
It just took me longer to leave this place.
Everything shifted—the way you look, the way you speak;
And for once, I no longer feel weak.

What we had back then, and what we have now,
They're night and day; I'm healed somehow.
Your responses faded, sometimes not there.
We once had attention, with intent to care.

But the fight for your presence has left me bare,
And the intention behind it vanished into thin air.
As much as I'd love to know who you are today,
It feels like meeting a stranger in some way.

I'm convinced you forced yourself to pull away,
So that you, too, could keep me at bay.
But I can, and I must, move on from this.
I'll shine my love where it's fully embraced,
where it's missed.

For today, I am certain, for the first time, it's true;
I am no longer in love with you. I wish you the best,
Take care as you go,
And thank you for letting me choose to let you go.

Though my love for you has finally passed;
I'll remember when it burned bright and clear.
For today, after such a long, long while;
I can finally say goodbye, and walk away with a smile.

—Sincerely Boris

The Last Poem I Wrote

I thought we were the kind of story
that would echo through decades,
carved into the backs of memory
like initials scratched into the tree we sat under.

There are things we never did,
like skipping stones across still waters,
or tending a small garden by a lake,
where our roots might have grown deep
in the quiet rhythm of earth and home.

We would have raised my daughter together,
woven laughter into days and years,
become a family in every small way,
with soft mornings and bedtime stories
that now only linger in my mind.

But all that remains is silence,
the space between two voices
that once believed they were one.

And even this friendship we're tending,
fragile as it is, won't survive the slow drift,
for time unthreads what's already loosening,
turning close bonds to distant memories.

One day we won't even get to say goodbye,
or share the peace of an ending,
our words lost, untethered,
like footprints washed from the shore.

You stand somewhere,
hand-in-hand with a new chapter,
and I imagine your eyes
finding their stead in a stranger's gaze.

How could love drift so far
from shared plans to this certainty?
That the future we sketched in quiet rooms
belongs now to the past,
a place I can no longer call home.

There is strength, they say, in release,
in loosening the grip,
not to keep or to cling,
but to bow with quiet grace
to what simply was.

—Sincerely, Boris

The Act of Learning Is, In Itself, An Act of Love; For Oneself, For Others, And for the World

While others stepped into their adult lives with degrees and institutional education, I leaned into curiosity, resourcefulness, and the need to prove that a lack of formal schooling could not define the boundaries of my potential.

My career in media and advertising became my classroom, each client challenge a case study, each meeting an opportunity to absorb. I approached the industry like an athlete studies a playbook, mastering its nuances, anticipating its moves, and finding new ways to elevate my craft.

But learning is not just about survival; it's about flourishing. Over the years, I've come to understand that the true mastery of learning lies not in amassing information, but in knowing how to retain, apply, and integrate it meaningfully into every corner of my life.

I've learned to ask myself: What does it mean to truly *understand* something? Not just to memorize it for a fleeting purpose, but to internalize it, to let it change me? Learning, I've found, is not a single act but a series of practices, much like meditation. It requires presence, patience, and purpose.

I have come to learn that lifelong learning starts with the right mindset. Every new skill or insight begins with belief;

belief that the effort is worthwhile, that failure is part of the process, and that growth often lies just beyond discomfort.

Early in my career, I felt the weight of imposter syndrome. Everyone around me seemed so confident, their credentials like badges of honor. I had to learn that my value came not from the letters after my name, but from my ability to adapt, to grow, and to contribute in meaningful ways.

This shift in mindset became a foundation not just for professional success, but for every personal challenge I've faced since: Surviving a toxic marriage, rebuilding my identity, and learning to be a father whose daughter sees strength in humility and perseverance.

There is immense power in focused attention. Learning deeply requires the discipline to focus; not just for minutes, but for sustained, meaningful stretches of time. In a world of constant distractions, this is a skill I had to cultivate. I remember times when a single pitch or client deadline demanded complete immersion. The clarity of thought that comes from deep work is incomparable; it carves pathways in the brain that shallow skimming never can.

Outside of work, I've applied this lesson to personal growth: Studying Buddhism taught me the value of single-pointed attention, whether through meditation or simply listening deeply during conversations. True focus, I've realized, is an act of care; for others and for oneself.

Through my learning journey, I have come to understand the importance of making space for repetition. One of the most practical lessons I've learned is that retention doesn't happen in one sitting. It's the repeated engagement with an idea—over days, weeks, or even years—that solidifies it in the mind. I see this now in the way I educate my daughter. We revisit lessons—not just new skills, problem solving, or reading, but values like resilience and kindness—through stories, shared experiences, and reflection.

In my professional life, this principle has shaped how I mentor colleagues. Revisiting a concept, reframing it, and finding new ways to apply it ensures that the learning sticks and evolves.

It's not enough to learn for learning's sake. Knowledge must be applied, tested, and lived. When I began studying feminism, it wasn't just to understand history or theory; it was to become a better advocate for my daughter to ensure she grows up seeing herself as equal, capable, and deserving of every opportunity.

Similarly, my recent exploration of art therapy wasn't an academic exercise; it was a way to process my own traumas and reconnect with my curiosity and creativity after struggling through mental, physical, financial, and emotional abuse throughout a fourteen-year relationship. These applications of learning have been deeply personal, but they've also enriched how I show up for others.

Through reflection, my understanding of my past, present, and future self has deepened. Journaling, storytelling, and conversations have been my tools for reflection. After each experience, whether a professional success, a personal failure, or a moment of quiet joy, I ask: *What did I learn? How did this change me?* This habit has turned my life into a tapestry of interconnected lessons, each thread woven with intention.

This reflective practice has been particularly important in parenting. When my daughter and I discuss her day or share a moment together, I see how these small acts of reflection build her emotional intelligence and deepen our bond.

To be a better colleague, I've learned to listen without judgment, to ask questions that spark insight, and to challenge my own biases. To be a better father, I've embraced patience, the art of asking instead of telling, and the joy of rediscovering the world through a child's eyes. To be a better friend and partner, I've worked on vulnerability: On showing my flaws and trusting others with them.

But most importantly, learning has been about becoming a better version of myself. I've faced darkness—mental health struggles, professional setbacks, and personal losses—but each challenge has been a teacher, shaping the man I am today and encouraging me to become the man I am destined to become.

The rewards of this journey are immeasurable. Professionally, it's allowed me to grow into a leader who inspires, uplifts, and puts people first. Personally, it's given me tools to heal, to connect, and to thrive. As a father, it's shown me how to model resilience and curiosity for my daughter. And most of all, it's taught me that the act of learning is, in itself, an act of love—for oneself, for others, and for the world.

My journey is far from over. Whether it's delving deeper into Buddhism, expanding and honoring my commitment to feminism, honing my skills in storytelling, or simply sitting with my daughter to explore her latest curiosity, I know that each step forward brings me closer to the life I aspire to live: One of meaning, connection, and endless growth.

—Sincerely, Boris

Final Chapter: Embracing The Path Forward

In a world of fleeting certainties, I have come to understand that true strength lies not in conquest but in the quiet resilience to adapt, to heal, and to ground myself. My journey has not been one of easy triumphs but of profound awakenings, a steady transformation driven by love, adversity, and the daily commitment to become more aligned with my true self. Through every hardship, loss, and moment of self-doubt, I have learned that destiny is not a distant achievement but a steady, unfolding revelation.

Each day begins with a ritual, a promise to myself: A meditation, a moment of gratitude, and a commitment to presence. These small practices are anchors, grounding me amid life's turbulence and reminding me that fulfillment is not found in the pursuit of perfection but in cultivating resilience and grace. The routines I keep, however simple, are less about control than about nurturing a relationship with my own heart, creating a foundation that allows me to approach each day with clarity and intention. The lessons I've learned are, in many ways, paradoxes: Finding strength in vulnerability, wisdom in uncertainty, and freedom in acceptance. I have come to embrace each part of myself, the light and the shadow, as essential elements of the whole. My life has taught me that to heal, I must face not only the wounds but also the parts of myself I once rejected. Self-compassion has become my compass, guiding me through the landscapes of my own doubts and insecurities. In learning to hold space for my imperfections, I have found the courage to stand more fully in my truth.

Fatherhood, more than any other role, has revealed the depths of this journey. My daughter has shown me that love's truest expression is presence, that strength is less about authority and more about offering a safe, nurturing space. Through her, I am reminded daily that love is built not in grand gestures but in the simple acts of being there, of listening, of showing up. In teaching her resilience, empathy, and self-worth, I have, in turn, learned to extend these same values to myself. But my role as her father is only one facet of a broader commitment: To live a life that honors my values, my heritage, and my journey. I carry with me the strength of the immigrant experience, the resilience forged through struggle and adaptation. This journey has taught me that fulfillment is not about arriving at a place of comfort but about growing continually into the person I am meant to be. It is about embracing life in its entirety, with all its uncertainties, losses, and, ultimately, the quiet moments of joy that lie beneath.

As I look back, I see a life shaped by both intention and surrender. There are paths I chose and others that were chosen for me, yet each has taught me the value of release; of letting go of the need for control and instead trusting that each experience, each moment, holds meaning. I have come to understand that the beauty of life lies not in the pursuit of a flawless narrative but in the raw, imperfect journey of self-discovery. My destiny, then, is not a place to reach but a life to be lived fully, a path walked with courage, humility, and an open heart. I move forward, not in pursuit of perfection, but in a commitment to growth, to presence, and to love. This journey, with all its triumphs and setbacks, has become a testament to the strength that lies in acceptance, to the wisdom that comes from enduring, and to the quiet power of choosing to live each day with integrity and intention. For as long as I am here, I will continue to evolve, to meet each day with gratitude, and to carry forward the love, the lessons, and the hope that have brought me to this moment. This is my legacy; a life lived with purpose, resilience, and an unwavering commitment to becoming the truest version of myself.

–

In the mirror's cold, indifferent stare,
I searched for a stranger who learned to bear
The weight of doubt, the scars of time,
The loss of light in a half-blind eye,
And a roadmap carved by surgeon's steel,
A testament to wounds that heal.
Fourteen years adrift in a loveless sea,
Tides of silence wore away at me.
I watched the man in glass turn gray;
Caged in choices, he would not stay.
He was cracked, uncertain, breaking slow,
Yet still, the only face I'd know.

I hid him well, that haunted frame,
Ashamed of his scars, his halting name.
But my daughter's laughter, light and wild,
Remade that man, unscarred and mild.
In her eyes, I found my shore,

A life worth living, forevermore.
Now each morning brings a truce,
A breath, a pen, a practiced use;
To see this face, and find some grace,
To honor the past and hold its place.
Through pain, through loss, a father learns,
To love the face that once he spurned.

So here I stand, a softened line,
With half a sight but a fuller mind,
And in the mirror's quiet, steady gaze,
I find the man I've learned to praise.
For all he's endured, for all he's done,
A father. A fighter. At last, one.

—Sincerely Boris

Note To Self:

Through the power of my thoughts and words,
incredible transformations are happening in me
and within my life right now.
I am worthy. I am grateful.
I am an unstoppable force of nature.

—Sincerely, Boris